Murder at the Star

Who killed Thomas Thomas?

For Ruth

and in gratitude to Annie Anthony (1923-2006)
and Margaret Deibert (1938-2007) for showing me how

Murder at the Star

Who killed Thomas Thomas?

Steve Adams

Seren is the book imprint of
Poetry Wales Press Ltd
Nolton Street, Bridgend, Wales

www.serenbooks.com
facebook.com/SerenBooks
Twitter: @SerenBooks

ISBN 978-1-78172-255-8
Mobi 978-1-78172-257-2
Epub 978-1-85411-256-5

A CIP record for this title is available from the British Library

The publisher works with the financial assistance
of the Welsh Books Council

Printed by Bell & Bain Ltd, Glasgow.

Contents

"I do not believe less than that the guilty one will eventually be discovered."
– John Nicholas, Coroner for the County of Carmarthenshire,
March 8, 1921

Prelude:
The Fat in the Fire

THE AMMAN VALLEY DERBY had become an increasing brutal and bloody affair during its nineteen history, stoked to boiling point by simmering feuds, neighbourly rivalries and bellies filled to bursting with booze and bitter hatred. Meetings between the valley's two premier rugby sides – Amman United and Ammanford – were a major event. Hundreds of supporters from both communities would flock to witness the spectacle where the anger and frustrations of a working week spent toiling at the coal-face spilled into enmity on and off the field. The contest between the sides on the cold, bright afternoon of Saturday, February 12, in 1921 was no different.

The fixture, the third and final meeting between the sides during the 1920/21 campaign, saw a crowd approaching 2,000 converge on Cwmaman Park on the border of the twin villages of Garnant and Glanaman, whose sportsmen combined to form United. The expectation amid even the most ardent of the visiting faithful was of a comfortable home victory as United looked to capitalise on their superior guile, skill and strength and put one over on the visitors from the small town just along the valley road. Ammanford had risen to become the dominant industrial and commercial power in the valley over the previous few decades and victory over them on the sporting field was a means to bring the swelling egos of its residents crashing down to earth. Nevertheless, a vast crowd made the five-mile journey east in buses, charabancs and on foot to cheer on their warriors in beer-fuelled expectation.

United, or The Amman as they were known, had crushed the visitors underfoot when the two sides met at Cwmaman Park early in the season and the odds were firmly stacked in their favour once again. Ammanford had claimed a most unlikely draw when the rivals had come together on their own patch just a few weeks earlier, but that result was seen as nothing but a blip – a fortunate result on home turf. This latest fixture would restore the natural order and Ammanford and their fans would be sent whimpering back home with tails fixed firmly between their legs.

There was however one chink in Amman's armour, and it came in the guise of their greatest player. William 'Billo' Rees was the valley's stand-out player of his generation. At outside-half he played the role of lynchpin between Amman's battling, bruising all-powerful front eight and their speedy, agile backs. Billo Rees was a midfield general – a visionary, fleet of foot and mind, dictating play and controlling possession from the centre of the park. Through him Amman played their game and outscored all-comers. Such was Billo's prowess with a leather oval ball in his hands that his talent had not gone unnoticed in the higher echelons of the Welsh rugby pyramid. Eventually he would pocket the silver pieces offered by the 13-man game of Rugby League in northern England, but even while still immersed in the union code of South Wales his fame had spread beyond the valley he called home.

On the day Ammanford and their masses rolled up at Cwmaman Park, Billo Rees had been selected to represent Swansea at the highest level of the Welsh amateur game. These were the days – at least officially – before a penny changed hands in the principality for pulling on a jersey on a Saturday after-noon. Though financial reward was not on offer – at least none that any would admit – still the major clubs were able to entice the shining lights from lower down the food-chain, and for smaller clubs like Ammanford and The Amman to see their players linking arms with the best the nation had to offer brought a sense of pride and its own prestige. The talents of men such as Billo Rees put villages like Garnant and Glanaman on the map. Players such as Billo were the source of their commu-nity's notion of self-worth and were heroes to their neighbours. The permit that was requested by Swansea though, was for once not met with favour amongst all The Amman fans, and contro-versy raged amongst the home support. Some labelled Rees a Judas, claiming he had turned his back on his own and money must surely have changed hands. When Ammanford arrived at

Cwmaman Park and their followers filled the Lamb and Flag, the Raven, the Cross Keys, the Salutation, the Prince Albert, the Half Moon, the Plough and Harrow, the Globe and every other pub in Garnant and Glanaman, there was hope. Small hope indeed, but without Billo Rees to orchestrate and marshal their superior forces, The Amman would not be at their best. There was a chance that the visitors might just win the day.

As the drinkers, home and away, their bellies stretched with ale, and whisky on their breath weaved their way through the crisp spring afternoon tempers flared and old rivalries from pub, pithead and pitch stirred amongst the jostling crowds of barging shoulders, pointed elbows and on occasion, flailing fists. Along the way, Police Sergeant Thomas Richards and Constable David Thomas, though lost in the surging crowds making their way to the field, did what they could to uphold order, through mere visible presence more than hands-on policing. As supporters began arriving at the ground they were met by a rumour which soon raged through the crowd like a summer wildfire on the sheep-shorn grasslands of Mynydd y Betws to the south and the Black Mountain to the north. Cheers of joy erupted amongst the home fans while fury raced through the visiting ranks. The word was out that Billo Rees had turned down the call from Swansea and whatever cash might be on offer, and instead had opted to spend that Saturday with The Amman. He had chosen to turn his back on greatness – or at least delay it – to crush the bitterest rivals of his neighbours. To the horror and disgust of many, Rees had rejected the far greater stage to ensure his home side smashed the hearts of Ammanford. It seemed a petty, bitter, spiteful choice. The decision, to travelling fans at least, was a betrayal: a betrayal of the very notion of sportsmanship; a betrayal of the hopes and aspirations of every player on every pitch in every village across South Wales. That The Amman had persuaded their shining light to reject the dreams to which all those who followed the amateur game aspired was beyond redemption. Anger crackled around Cwmaman Park and shoves, sneers and pushes spilled over into punches, kicks and full-blown fights. "The fat was properly in the fire," reported Sentinel, the *Amman Valley Chronicle's* rugby correspondent.

For the players of Ammanford Rugby Football Club, the

Billo Rees controversy brought far greater, and more immediate concerns. They knew that whatever the bitter atmosphere amongst the crowds that pressed tight and 30 deep around the touchlines, they would have to face the genius on the field and somehow suppress him. To a man, they all knew without doubt, that Billo's talent far surpassed their own; his speed of thought, vision and awareness of the field around him would leave them floundering in the mud as The Amman raced out of sight to yet another victory. They knew also that such was his talent they would be lucky to ever find themselves within an arm's reach of him. The genius that was Billo Rees was simply head and shoulders above them all and far too good for any to ever lay an off-the-ball punch, let alone a legal tackle on him. And so it was that the captain of the Ammanford XV opted for a different approach.

The role of outside-half which Billo had so mastered is the key link in a chain. It is the fundamental position which unites the two disparate sections of a rugby union side. A team is made up of 15 players: numbers one to eight make up the pack while numbers nine to 15 form the back division. The pack are big, strong men who bind together when a scrum is called, who form a receiving line when the ball is returned to play after going off the field. The pack is the blunt instrument, the brutal, pounding hammer designed to wear down the opposition and sap their strength and will. The backs meanwhile spread out across the park. They provide the incisive scalpel cuts to the front-eight's hammer blows. The role of outside-half – the number ten position – is the pivot between the creaking, groaning brutes of the pack and charging centres, flying wingers and graceful full-backs.

The Amman's muscular, relentless pack would claim every ball in scrum or ruck and feed it out to the number nine, scrum-half Joe Griffiths. Griffiths' single purpose on the field was to ensure he offered up clean, unimpeded ball to Rees. Rees meanwhile, would linger ten yards to the rear of the forwards' melee and from that point of freedom release his rampaging backs to leave Ammanford chasing ghosts. As they tied their bootlaces and pulled on their jerseys, the Ammanford game plan began to take shape. It was a plan so daring, so unpredicted, so unlikely, that none in The Amman's ranks could have seen it coming. The Ammanford captain ordered his side to ignore the genius Rees and leave him wander how and where he wished. Billo Rees, the most feared and talented rugby player of his generation, was to be given the complete freedom of Cwmaman Park. Instead the entire Ammanford team were to focus their brutal attentions on Griffiths – a talented player in his own right, but far short of the imperious standard of Rees and without the physique and mental ingenuity of his three-quarter line partner. Ammanford would target Griffiths and batter him into the ground. Two, three, often four men at a time would converge on him before he was able even to scoop up the ball up from the back of the scrum. Ammanford would crush him under flying bodies, flailing arms and heavy, studded boots – and in so doing would break the chain at its weakest link.

The tactic sent the home fans apoplectic and yet more fights broke out along the sidelines. The mood both on the field and off turned ugly. Talent, skill and prowess with a ball were all cast to one side. Billo Rees enjoyed barely a touch of the ball all afternoon as Joe Griffiths became a lamb to the visitors' slaughter. Ammanford claimed a historic and infamous 10-8 victory. The mood along the Amman Valley spat and fizzed throughout the remainder of the afternoon and on into the night. The fat indeed was in the fire.

PART ONE

Chapter One:
An awful scream and then a thud

AT 8.15PM ON SATURDAY, February 12, 1921, and with the last customers of the day finally departed, shop manager Thomas Thomas locked the door at the front of the branch of Star Stores in the Carmarthenshire mining village of Garnant. He turned the sign which hung in the window from Open to Closed and pulled down the blind to signal the end of the day's business. Fifteen-year-old John Morris, one of the shop's two full-time teenage delivery boys and general assistants, fixed in place the portable gate at the mouth of the porch into which was set the main customer entrance between the two large bay display windows and returned inside via the side doorway accessed down the narrow dark passage between the Star and Mrs Smith's fruit shop next door. Mr Thomas inspected the board he had fixed over the cracked pane in the window to the left of the store which through his own clumsiness he had broken earlier in the day while attempting rearrange the display. He had cursed himself as the cans had fallen, though not in any way which might offend the Lord. Having assessed the situation following the breakage, he had sent Trevor Morgan, the thirteen-year-old errand boy who worked at the Star on Saturdays, to the cellar at the rear of the store to find a suitable piece of wood with which he had covered the damage and secured the window until a tradesman could be engaged and a more permanent solution arranged on Monday morning.

While Mr Thomas checked the board was fixed firmly in place against the broken pane and would remain secure throughout the night and all day Sunday when the store would remain closed, Phoebe Jones – the first assistant at the Star – and grocery assistant Helena 'Nellie' Richards began weighing up the stock as was the custom at the close of business each day. Phoebe had already pulled down the blinds on the grocery counter window and once the board was in place, Mr Thomas did the same behind the provisions counter. The boy Morris and the other full-time general assistant, fourteen-year-old Emlyn Richards, began to clear up after a busy day's trading, sweeping the floor and tidying away discarded packaging. Both boys were glad of their positions at the Star as it saved them – or at least delayed them – from the otherwise inevitable career of a life spent underground. Emlyn however, was less than overjoyed to spend each day being ordered around by his elder sister Nellie, both at home and at work. With the window finally as secure as was possible under the circumstances, Thomas Thomas went to the safe in the small storage area at the rear of the store which was stacked on top with tins of condensed milk and jars of marmalade, and removed the account books and the two old biscuit tins in which he would place whatever cash was to be kept at the store overnight. Leaving the safe door open, he took both tins and the ledgers back into the shop and, with Nellie having already cleared the surface, placed them on the grocery counter where he began calculating the day's takings, totalling the cash and receipts, and balancing the customer accounts books. Business has been brisk throughout the day. The big rugby match was of no interest to the shop manager, but the exceptionally large crowd which had swarmed into the little mining village to cheer on the opposing sides in the Amman Valley derby was warmly welcomed. The day had proved particularly profitable for the Star and its manager was greatly pleased by the cash which had kept the tills ringing throughout the afternoon and evening. Thomas Thomas was a man of devout belief. He frowned upon anything other than strict abstinence, but was certainly not averse to taking the money of those men and women who indulged in the demon drink. Indeed, it was better – to the mind of Thomas Thomas at least – that the weak-minded sinners spent their money at the Star rather than in one of the many alehouses that flourished in the valley.

At 8.45pm, Nellie Richards, having sought and received the permission of Mr Thomas, ran a hasty errand for Miss Jones. She raced past the open safe and down the fourteen steps from the storeroom into the cellar where empty boxes and unused odds and ends were stored. Although the cellar had no light of its own, Nellie could see well enough by the light cast down the steps from the shop and she left the Star by the rear basement door. The seventeen-year-old was gone no more than a few minutes, having merely stepped next door to Commerce House, where Miss Jones lodged, to enquire as to the progress of repairs being made to her colleague's favourite dress. Phoebe Jones had plans for the evening and had already been granted the permission of Mr Thomas to leave work a few minutes early that night. She aimed to finish up her daily tasks as quickly as she was able, race home to Commerce House and change into her best outfit so that she might attend that evening's concert at Stepney Hall in the company of a close friend.

With Nellie expecting to be gone no more than a minute or two, she left the rear door of the Star ajar. It had remained unlocked throughout the day as usual, with numerous customers leaving the store by the rear entrance. Those who wished to avoid the extra charge for having their goods delivered often came down the steps and selected a box to carry home their purchases and then made their way out by way of the cellar door before turning right and passing along the rear of Mrs Smith's fruit shop then heading up into Coronation Arcade and back onto the main valley road. Upon her return, Nellie pulled the back door shut and secured it using its two standard sliding bolts. For added security, an iron bar, which was kept behind the door, was positioned across the frame. Nellie's younger brother, standing at the top of the stairs, paused from his task of sweeping the back room to watch her as she fixed the bar. It was usually his final task of the day. With the door closed and firmly locked, Nellie climbed the fourteen steps from the basement into the room at the rear of the shop and confirmed to Miss Jones that Mrs Jeffreys was progressing well with the stitching repairs and that the dress would be ready to wear in time for arrival back at Commerce House. Only after Nellie had secured the door and returned upstairs did her brother and Trevor Morgan finish their cleaning, sweeping the last of the floors and scooping up their various piles of dirt and detritus from the day into a small box which they then carried down the steps and placed on the floor against the wall between the cellar door and the rear window that looked out down towards the River Amman and the row of houses known as Arcade Terrace. The window was too thickly coated in dust to see through, but in the day-time the light from the sun gave it a warm glow, while after dark the lights from inside the store could be seen clearly from outside. The two boys went back up the steps and Emlyn Richards returned the broom to its usual resting place, leaning against the wall alongside the safe in the storeroom at the top of the stairs. Mr Thomas was meticulous in his approach to the management of the store and the boys knew only too well that the box of floor shavings, the broom and a host of other items were to be placed exactly where expected if they were to escape the shopkeeper's wrath and yet another sermon from the pages of the Good Book.

At 8.50pm, Nellie Richards and the three boys, with their tasks completed for the day, bade their goodnights to Miss Jones and Mr Thomas and left the shop by the side door behind the provisions counter. Once through the first internal door they walked along the dank, unlit passage and out through the external door which brought them into the night air on the main valley road. The door was supposed to be used exclusively by staff, but they were aware that on a few rare occasions, regular customers arriving after hours had been permitted to enter when in need of some forgotten ingredient necessary for their supper. As Nellie and the boys left they ensured that the door onto the street was pulled shut and the latch engaged. On the main road all was dark save for the lights cast by the shops of Commerce Place. Street-lighting would take another two years to arrive in Cwmaman. The street was growing quiet after the hustle and bustle of the day. The men who had spent the afternoon at the match were in the pubs and would remain there for another hour or two while the women were at home, preparing supper for husbands and sons who had spent the day at the colliery or the tinworks, or those still in the pub. The Richards siblings walked together eastwards towards their home at Garnant Police Station where their father was the village sergeant. The boys Morris and Morgan each went their separate ways to their families.

With the store's junior staff departed, Thomas Thomas and Phoebe Jones continued settling the day's accounts and completing the final chores of the weekend. The following day was

Sunday, when the only businesses enjoying brisk trade would be the many chapels that lined the South Wales valleys. At 9.45pm, Phoebe finally swapped her work apron for her coat and said goodnight to her manager. Mr Thomas had frowned upon her request to leave a little early – and certainly disapproved of her plans for the evening, however, despite the staunchness of views on the consumption of alcohol, loose attitudes and his adherence to the word of the Good Book, he was a kindly enough man. His permission for her early departure had been accompanied by a short sermon on clean living, but nonetheless it had been granted. As she made her way to the side door, Phoebe paused and looked down from the top the staircase. The February night cast dark shadows in odd shapes around the boxes piled on top of one another in the cellar and into the corners of the darkened room, but there was still sufficient illumination from the shop and storage area gaslights to ensure she could clearly see that the rear door was bolted shut and secured with the iron bar.

As was her habit, she turned back to Mr Thomas to confirm that the rear of the shop was locked up. Her manager, still pouring over the shop ledgers on the grocery counter, expressed his thanks and wished her a pleasant evening. Alongside the account books were the two cash tins. After balancing the tills from the grocery and provisions counters, Thomas Thomas would separate the money into two neat piles, one of Treasury notes and the other of the coins. He would then place the paper money – after it had been bundled into clear amounts – into the smaller of the tins. The silver coins meanwhile would be placed into the larger tin, the coppers returned to the tills to form the float. The smaller tin containing the notes would then be placed inside the larger.

The shopkeeper's final task of the day – to be carried out just moments before he too swapped apron for jacket and overcoat – would be to place the tins inside the safe for the remainder of the weekend. As Phoebe took one final glance into the storage area she could see that the safe door was wide open, as it would remain until Mr Thomas locked it with the key which had sat in the safe door keyhole all day. Once the safe was locked, the shop manager would place the key in his pocket – along with the key to the side door padlock, which he would fix to the staff entrance once he too had left the building for the night. Phoebe Jones stepped out of the side door and into the Carmarthenshire night at just a minute or two after 9.45pm, the only lights which remained were those burning at the Star and at the fruit shop next door, which would be open for another 30 minutes. Thomas Thomas meanwhile remained behind the grocery counter, struggling to make sense of one small discrepancy in his figures. The miscalculation annoyed him, but not greatly so as he totalled up what had, by any measure, been an excellent day's trading.

At 10.15pm – some 30 minutes after Phoebe Jones had left the Star Stores for the night, Diana Bowen filled her basket with a few potatoes, a carrot or two, an onion and a few apples from the display boxes in Fanny Smith's fruit shop at Number Three, Commerce Place. She was the last customer of the day. She would also be the only adult witness to the murder at the Star. Diana paid the few shillings that were due and said her goodnights to Mrs Smith, the proprietor, and shop assistant Alice Stammers before ushering her two young daughters – Catherine and Elsie – to the door. Diana was all too aware that she was already running very late. The 33-year-old would have to hurry if she was to get home in time to have a hot supper ready for her husband David when he arrived home exhausted from another ten-hour shift as a stoker at the nearby Gellyceidrim colliery. Diana pulled her girls out into the street where a fine mist was settling and beginning to thicken. The day had been unseasonably warm, but the temperature had fallen sharply with the arrival of darkness and a hard frost nipped at the children's faces. The road and muddy fields around the village had already turned rock hard in the cold night and the pavement was turning icy under foot. The main road through the village, which in time would become known as Cwmaman Road but in 1921 was still referred to simply as the valley road, had quietened considerably over the past few hours, but would soon be springing back to life as the men made their way home from the Gellyceidrim, Raven and the other smaller collieries and the tinworks. There were still a few people on the street as Diana and her girls left Mrs Smith's fruit shop and set off westwards on the short walk towards home. Here and there wives and mothers rushed for late-night provisions to feed tired husbands and sons who soon, like David Bowen, would be heading home from the pit once the end-of-shift hooter blew. Most of the men who had worked the morning shift were still in one of the many village pubs, reliving the agonies of the afternoon's big derby where Ammanford had caused such outrage by their underhand tactics.

Diana and the girls had taken no more than a few steps along the slippery pavement towards the small rooms they called home at Northampton Buildings when they were halted in their tracks by a most ungodly noise from within Star Supply Stores, the upmarket national chain which occupied Number Two, Commerce Place, next door to Fanny Smith's fruit shop.

"It was an awful screech," Diana would later tell a reporter from the *Amman Valley Chronicle*.

"I was standing on the pavement a few feet away from the window of the stores.

"I heard an awful screech and the sound of boxes being moved about. There was a thud and the sound of running feet – as if someone was running upstairs. The children with me heard the noises as well, and were frightened."

Elsie, the youngest Bowen girl at nine years, may have been frightened, but she was an inquisitive child by nature and it would require more than just a screech to staunch her curiosity. She rushed to the window and peered inside to discover what had gone on behind the drawn-down blinds of the shop's frontage.

"She said she had seen nothing inside but tins of condensed milk," said her mother later. "It would have been about 10.15pm when I heard that dreadful noise. At 10.30pm I was at home preparing supper in our own house."

However, some three weeks later at the inquest into the death of Mr Thomas Thomas, branch manager at the Star Supply Stores, she put the time of the dreadful shriek more precisely, at exactly 10.20pm.

"It was such an awful scream," she told Sergeant Thomas Richards the day after the incident as he tried to piece together the murderous events of the previous evening with what limited information was available. Sergeant Richards, the father of

Nellie and Emlyn – the two young assistants at the Star – was the highest-ranking officer based at Garnant Police Station. Diana would go on to tell the inquest jury that the scream had startled her and that she thought it strange, but said that she had made no attempt to see beyond the blinds or look inside the shop's interior. She admitted that she had made no effort to discover the cause of such a fearful scream.

"I was going to have a look," she said, "but after hearing running on the stairs I thought everything was all right."

"The scream was a loud one, but it gradually died away and then all was calm afterwards. I thought the boy in the shop had had his hand in the bacon-slicing machine, which was on the counter nearest to the side I was standing. I know that he had done it before. Everything was quiet when we left."

The momentary distraction over, Diana Bowen pulled her girls away and made for home, her mind again now focussed on the return of her husband. Not one other soul in Garnant had heard the awful sound save Diana and her daughters – well none who might ever admit to it. Despite her haste to make for home and begin the task of cooking, Diana did somehow find the time to pause briefly to chat when she saw two neighbours – Mrs Michael and Mrs Walters – making their way towards her on the opposite side of the valley road. Though she was so very late – too late to stop and check on the occupants of the Star – she found time to tell her neighbours of the scare she had just suffered.

"I told them that I had had a fright and that the boy had caught his hand in the bacon machine," said Diana. "I told them everything was all right now."

She only stopped once more and then not until she had reached Northampton Buildings where she met Mrs Smith, another neighbour, on the doorstep. Again she put on hold all thought of her husband's impending arrival to relay her tale of the dreadful noise and the boy with his hand in the bacon slicer one final time. Then, at last, she went inside and set about preparing supper. All was deathly quiet behind the blinds of Star Stores when Diana Bowen and her girls left the arc of light cast from the gas lamps behind the shutters onto the pavement outside the shop. All was quiet behind the blinds of Star Stores at Two Commerce Place in Garnant, because Thomas Thomas, the manager, was already in the grasp of death.

At the very moment that Diana Bowen was regaling Mrs Michael and Mrs Walters with her tale of awful screams and bacon slicers, another Garnant resident was down along the floor of the valley basin some way to the rear of Commerce Place. William Charles Brooks, one of the many men who had arrived in the valley seeking a regular pay packet a decade earlier, was dreaming of his own hot supper after his shift as a beater at the Amman Tinplate Works came to a close. His day's work over, Brooks had left the tinworks and crossed the Great Western Railway line before making his way along Arcade Terrace, a row of houses in the valley's dip behind the shops, to his home at Number Four. Brooks, a 32-year-old Londoner by birth, had settled in Garnant around 1910 and married Mary Ann Harries – quite possibly with a shotgun at his head. Baby Henrietta had died before she reached six months – and long before her parents had the opportunity – or the right – to celebrate their first anniversary – but Nelly had soon followed and William junior too.

As Brooks made his way past his mother-in-law's house at Number Two, Arcade Terrace, he glanced up at the rear of the shops and the dim glow emanating from the properties that lined the valley road which he could see through Coronation Arcade. The Arcade, which in turn had given his own terraced row its name, ran at ground level between Numbers Four and Five, Commerce Place. Number Four was the second of the two drapers shops in the row belonging to Williams and Harries – the partnership between two former valley rivals had benefitted both and their booming business had seen them occupy Numbers One and Four, sandwiching Star Stores and Fanny Smith's fruit shop in the block. Both drapers shops were in darkness but Brooks could see lights still burning upstairs in the fruit shop and at the rear of the Star.

As he looked he saw a figure lurking in the shadows of the Arcade. It made no move towards the street, but stayed half hidden within the folds of darkness as if watching and listening. From the valley road he was all but invisible, but Brooks was able to make him out. The man appeared to be waiting for any sound or movement that might be made out on the main highway beyond William Brooks' sight or hearing. The shadows cast by the shop-lights which ensured his invisibility from the road only served to enhance the definition of his form from Brooks' lowly point of observation in the valley basin. The man, Brooks realised, was Morgan Walter Jeffreys, the landlord of Commerce Place, the man who had built the row of shops from nothing, and who revelled in the position such importance granted him. Eventually the figure turned and, facing Brooks though clearly unaware of his presence, made his way down to the end of the Arcade before turning left, following the line of the buildings along back of the drapers, fruit shop and the Star to Commerce House, the residential property set behind the first of the Williams and Harries shops.

Sometime after 10pm, but certainly before 10.30pm, Anne Jeffreys opened the rear door of Commerce House and sent Spot the family dog outside to go about his nightly business. The rear of Commerce Place was quiet and Mrs Jeffreys neither saw nor heard anything she might consider untoward. She went back inside and left Spot in privacy. Within minutes however, her quiet peace was shattered as the dog roused her from her chair beside the fire.

"Spot barked furiously," Mrs Jeffreys told Sergeant Richards the following day.

"As everything was so quiet outside I shouted to the dog: 'What's the matter boy?'"

The 61-year-old was all alone in the house, but was not one to be shaken easily. Although it was her husband who had overseen construction and who managed the current tenants of Commerce Place, it was Anne who entered into discussions with Lord Dynevor over a lease for the land. It was Anne who, on July 13, 1895, finally reached agreement with the land-owner, and signed the lease for the vacant plot from which would one day spring what she had every hope might become a retail empire. The lease remained in Anne's name until she signed it over to her husband on August 29, 1903. However, it was Anne who would remain the named defendant in a twenty year legal dispute with the Dynevor Estate. The wrangle – over financial responsibility for the costs incurred by the essential improvements required on the valley road – saw Anne and her husband refuse to pay a single penny of the agreed ground-rent until ordered to do so by a High Court ruling following a bitter battle with Walter FitzUryan Rice, the seventh Baron Dynevor, in July 1915. The legal costs alone had, in truth, all but bankrupted the Jeffreys. Anne however had refused to be intimidated by the Baron's lawyers and friends in the judiciary. She was certainly not a woman afraid of the dark. She went to the door to see what had so riled the dog, but saw nothing she considered to be obviously out of the ordinary.

"I could see nothing so I called the dog to come in," she said. "Spot then came in, so I forgot everything about it."

At precisely 10.30pm, Fanny Smith and Alice Stammers, having dealt with the few last late-comers, locked the front door of the fruit shop at Number Three, Commerce Place, and pulled down the shutters on the windows. With business finally over for the day the two women went upstairs to their living quarters and settled down to supper. They would – as usual – return to the shop later to clear away the rubbish of the day. Like so many of the residents of Garnant, neither Fanny nor Alice was a native. Fanny Mansfield had been born in Bath in 1869 and at the age of twenty-five was swept of her feet by a smooth-talking travelling fruit salesman from Wolverhampton by the name of William Henry Smith. They married in the summer of 1894 and in little over a year, a son – Raymond – was born. All was not well with their new-born however and Raymond was classed as "paralysed at birth" – quite possibly a Victorian diagnosis for cerebral palsy. For a time at least – and quite possibly because of Raymond's condition – the Smith family settled in Bristol. William continued his life as a commercial travelling salesman while Fanny remained at home with Raymond and Phillip, the family's latest addition. Phillip had arrived in the early months of 1901 and would be the Smith's only other child. The family had however also gained another – albeit unofficial – member by the time Phillip had been born. The couple had taken on a general maid to help relieve the pressure on Fanny while William was "on the road". Alice Stammers was a Londoner, born in 1878, and by 1901 was already a fixture in the Smith household. She would remain at Fanny's side for half a century until the death of her employer in 1950, but her devotion would go unrewarded and unrecognised. She received not one penny of the £2,400 nest egg Fanny Smith had accumulated prior to her death.

By 1911, William too had tired of the life of a travelling salesman and, with Fanny, Phillip and Alice joining him, had set up in business running a fruit shop in Sale, Cheshire. Raymond meanwhile had been placed in the care of a residential school for epileptic children close by at Nether Alderley. Life in the north of England did not go especially well for the Smiths however and by the middle of the decade they had returned to Bristol, where Raymond died aged 23 in the latter months of 1918. Soon after the death of their eldest son, the Smith family moved again, taking up the tenancy of a vacant shop in the village of Garnant. Alice would help out in the shop as well as with the household's domestic chores. William returned to the life he knew best – on the road as a travelling salesman and fruit wholesaler.

Each night, with the day's work done, the two women would lock the shop at 10.30pm and go upstairs where they would for a short time settle down to eat their main meal of the day in a room at the rear of the first floor of Number Three, Commerce Place. The room overlooked the rear gardens of the row and down towards Arcade Terrace. Further still, on a clear night, they could see across the GWR railway line, to where the lights still burned at the Amman Tin Works. Beyond them, in the inky blankness past the sight of Fanny Smith and Alice, rolled the River Amman. As the two women ate their meal on the night of February 12, 1921, they heard not a sound nor saw any movement whatsoever at the rear of Commerce Place. They heard no barking dogs, no shouts, no awful screams, nor any music in the night, and they most certainly did not see a killer making his escape from the rear of the building next door. At 12.45am, Fanny Smith and Alice Stammers could put off their final chores no more. The two women returned downstairs to the fruit shop and cleared up the empty boxes, the wrapping paper and the leaves and vegetation left over from the day's trading. Both noticed however that despite the lateness of the hour and the arrival of the Sabbath, the lights within Star Stores still burned brightly.

Thomas Walter Jeffreys had clocked off work at Cawdor

Colliery at 10pm after another arduous eight-hour shift at the coal-face and begun to make the slow trudge home. By the time he reached Commerce House, passing to the rear of Fanny Smith's fruit shop, Harries and Williams drapers and the cellar door of Star Stores, it was as close to 10.30pm as made no difference. Thomas, at 26, was the youngest – and more respectable – son of Morgan and Anne Jeffreys, landlords of Commerce Place. When interviewed by the *Amman Valley Chronicle* in the days after the murder at the Star, Thomas claimed he had noticed nothing out of the ordinary on his way home that night. Perhaps he was too tired or too hungry; perhaps it was because of the heavy mist that was thickening and settling in the valley by the time he got home that evening, but for whatever reason he said that he had not spotted the lights still burning at Star Stores.

"I noticed nothing then but that the back door was closed," he told the newspaper's reporter. The only thing he thought he had noticed was in fact wrong. However, when interviewed by police in the days that followed, his recollection of the evening proved somewhat different.

"I noticed a light on in the Star Stores as I was passing through the back," he told Sergeant Richards. He was in no doubt that he had noticed it as he had gone so far as to comment on the shopkeeper's long hours on his arrival home.

Once inside Commerce House, Thomas settled down in the kitchen to eat the supper prepared for him by his mother. There he said he remained until Phoebe Jones, the first assistant at Star Stores, arrived home at her lodgings from the concert at Stepney Hall a little after 11pm. Phoebe certainly had noticed that the lights were still burning and praised – though possibly with a snort of derision – the dedication of her manager, who she assumed was still struggling to pinpoint the minor discrepancy in his accounts. At around 11.30pm, Thomas and his father set out across the fields to the stables which they kept nearby to "bed the ponies for the night". As they made their way back to Commerce House they again noted that the lights were still burning throughout the store, but saw no reason for alarm. By the time father and son had arrived back home, Phoebe was nowhere to be seen. Mrs Jeffreys told them she had gone to check on Mr Thomas at the Star, though she can have been gone for no more than a few minutes. Morgan Jeffreys went to bed while Thomas settled back into his seat alongside his mother.

When Phoebe returned she told them that Mr Thomas must have left the lights burning and gone home for the night. She praised his conscientiousness in relation to his dedication to the company, but admitted that he could, on occasion, be rather absent-minded. She asked where Mr Jeffreys was as he might wish her to fetch the shop manager rather than leave the lights burning all night, but Anne told her that her husband was already in his bed. Phoebe went to bed herself a short time after, as did Mrs Jeffreys. Thomas remained at the kitchen hearth, alone with his thoughts. He later claimed that it was while he sat watching the flames engulf the black coal which sustained this village and so many others like it that he wondered whether such a man so careful as Mr Thomas might deliberately have left the gas lights burning in a bid to deter any would-be burglars. He was aware that a window in the store had been broken earlier in the day and was only loosely boarded up with wood. Thomas told himself that burglars might well view the broken window as an open invitation and to leave the gas lights burning through the night was a prudent decision, yet he was to keep such thoughts to himself until called before the Coroner's court some three weeks later. Though even when he recalled his fire-side thoughts for the jury, he did not explain how exactly he had been made aware of the broken window as he had been at work all day and evening. It may be that his father told him, or his mother or Phoebe on her return, but none was to ever make reference to any such conversation.

At 12.45pm Morgan Powell Jeffreys, Thomas' elder brother arrived back at Commerce House "the worse for drink". Morgan had been oblivious to the goings-on around him as he stumbled home and had completely failed to notice that the lights at Star Stores were still burning. Perhaps it was his experiences on the battlefields of northern France, where he served throughout the Great War as a Private in the Welsh Regiment that nourished his liking for a drink. Perhaps it was his nature. Or perhaps it was the decision of Cwmaman parish leaders to omit him from a concert in honour of the serving troops when he returned home on weekend leave in November 1916, it was, after all, the second time he had suffered such a slight at the hands of his own community. Perhaps it was his reputation which garnered such an oversight. The *Amman Valley Chronicle* certainly found his twice-suffered indignity improper. Whatever the feelings of the community towards a single individual, the young men who went and fought deserved respect and gratitude. "Please treat them all alike," the valley paper urged in a plea to give Morgan Jeffreys the recognition he deserved. Whatever his reasons, Morgan Powell Jeffreys liked a drink, and when he made his way home during the early hours of February 13, 1921, he certainly had no clue as to whether the rear cellar door of Star Stores was open or what lights might or might not still be burning.

"I waited up for my brother then locked the door," Thomas later said. "I am quite sure my brother did not say anything about the lights being on."

Thomas served his brother supper and then both men retired for the night, one exhausted from his toils, the other swimming in a haze of beer.

A night out at Stepney Hall may well have been a birthday treat for Phoebe, who turned 30 in February, 1921. A tall, thin woman with angular features, Phoebe, like Thomas Thomas, was born in the village of Llangendeirne, though she had taken up employment at Garnant in 1917 – two years before Thomas Thomas arrived to take over as manager. Miss Jones had got on very well with the previous manager Mr Lewis and by the time Mr Thomas arrived in 1919 she was the most senior member of staff other than the manager himself. Though both hailed from the small village some 18 miles west of Garnant, it is unlikely that they would have known each prior to Thomas Thomas arriving in Garnant. Phoebe, however, would undoubtedly have known the Thomas family and most likely would have had the shoes she wore in childhood repaired by his father.

She had raced through her end-of-day duties as fast as she was able and at 9.45pm left Mr Thomas alone in the shop. The concert finished at 11pm and Phoebe made her way back along the valley road to Commerce House and her lodgings with the Jeffreys family. As she passed Commerce Place she could not help but notice that the lights were still burning behind the blinds at the Star. When she arrived home, she remarked how strange it was that the manager was still working so late on a Saturday night, particularly in light of his devotion to the Bible and the teachings of the chapel. The day of rest, in the eyes of Mr Thomas, was the Lord's Day and not a day for the betterment of the Star Tea Company, no matter how devoted an employee he may be.

"Fancy Mr Thomas in the shop now," she told Thomas Jeffreys upon arriving home. "Whatever is the matter with the man? He must be shop mad."

However, Phoebe felt a growing unease and at 11.25pm went to investigate. From the back door of Commerce House, she could see the glow of the Star Store lights shining through the dusty cellar window. She passed behind the rear of the shops, up through the arcade and out to the front of Star Stores. The lights in the shop were still burning just as they had been when she had passed previously. She, like the youngest Bowen girl a little over an hour earlier, peered through the window, trying to glimpse around the lowered blinds to look inside. She could see no movement in the shop. As she positioned herself to get a better view into the building she spotted Mr Thomas' white shop jacket and apron hanging next to some sides of bacon on a rack at the rear of the shop. There was no sign of Thomas Thomas. Initially she wondered whether he might still be in the back room or in the upstairs warehouse, but when she heard no sound she assumed he must have gone home having forgotten to switch off the lights.

"Though," she admitted later, "this would have been a most unusual course."

Glanyrafon Villas was a row of semi-detached properties at the top of Horney Road on the opposite side of the valley to the Star. Separated from the throng by the GWR train lines, the tinplate works, the River Amman and then the recreation ground and rugby pitches where the Amman Valley derby had been played out earlier in the day, the development of nine houses was set apart from the village. From its elevated position, Glanyrafon Villas looked down on the bustle of the valley road with an aloof eye. It was at the fringes of the community. So too were the people who called it home. At Number Two, Thomas Charles Hooper Mountstephens lived with his wife Lily, his sons Arthur and William, and two lodgers: Thomas Thomas, the current manager of the Star Stores, and Arthur Impey, a chess-loving cockney miner whose childhood read like a Dickens novel.

Impey was born within earshot of Bow bells in West Ham in 1888, the second of three children. Mere existence had been a struggle for the Impeys: David, Arthur's father, brought home only a labourer's meagre wage. Life was extremely hard for the Impey children in the slums of east London, but it was about to get much, much worse. On November 25, 1892, David Impey died aged 45. Less than seven months later, he was followed into the ground by his wife, Ellen. She was just 42. On June 18, 1893, the three Impey children were made orphans. Arthur was five, sister Ellen 12 and Albert just two. Despite the hardships, Ellen had some money. When she died she left £82 and 9 shillings. Where she came by it is unknown. It was not a fortune, but certainly it was a sum of money. Ellen's Last Will and Testament left everything to a woman named Charlotte Elizabeth Housdon. The nature of Housdon's relationship to Ellen Impey remains uncertain as there is no record that they were sisters or in any way related, as does the question of whether the money came with an unspoken – or at least unwritten – obligation that the recipient should care for the three Impey children. Whatever the logic and expectations behind Ellen's bequest, the children did not spend any length of time with the Housdons, and the Impeys – as a family – dissolved forever.

By 1901, Arthur, now thirteen, was an inmate at Muller's Orphan House in Bristol. How long he had been there as a resident is unknown, but he would not stay at Muller's much beyond his fourteenth birthday. At some point he made his way west – presumably in search of work. He settled in the Amman valley. By 1921, the workhouse orphan was employed at Gellyceidrim colliery. He was 33 years old and in love: Arthur would marry fiancée Blodwen Jones in Garnant before the year was out. In the meantime however, he remained in lodgings. Renting a room at Number Two, Glanyrafon Villas, meant renting a bed, or rather a share of a bed – a necessity in rural Wales where the number of paying lodgers far outweighed the available sleeping quarters. The Cwmaman community had more than doubled in less than 20 years and risen five-fold during the past half-century. Demand for housing far outstripped supply. Arthur shared a bed with Thomas Thomas, the frail, Bible-quoting little shopkeeper. Prior to Thomas' arrival in Garnant, Impey had shared that same bed with Mr Lewis, his current sleeping-partner's predecessor at the Star.

Arthur Impey's landlord, Thomas Charles Hooper Mountstephens, was also a Londoner. He was born in St Pancras in the centre of the great metropolis in the summer of 1886; the son of a piano tuner. By 1910 he, Lily and baby Arthur had escaped the city and were already living in Garnant. Their second son William arrived in 1911. Mountstephens was not afraid of hard toil and worked as a pumpman below ground at Gellyceidrim Colliery before moving up the mining career-ladder to become a fitter. However, he remained a distant figure from the majority of his colleagues at the colliery. Rather than frequent the local pubs and billiards halls with most of the men, he spent his free time reading and playing chess. His passion for the game saw him instrumental in the creation of the Cwmaman Chess Club, which – after a number of false starts and rescheduled meetings – held its first event the week before the murder of his lodger. Thomas Mountstephens was elected chairman of the club, Arthur Impey was also a paid up member.

At 11pm on Saturday, February 12, 1921, Thomas Mountstephens and his wife ate supper. It was normal in the valley to take supper – the main meal of the day – late, to match the changing shift patterns endured by the men who spent their day sweating underground. The Mountstephens' two sons had been fed earlier in the evening and were already asleep. Neither of the lodgers who paid for bed and board at Glanyrafon Villas had yet returned from their respective jobs though Arthur Impey would soon be trudging up the hill out of the mist at the end of his shift. Thomas Thomas had warned of his intention to work well beyond the usual hour when Mountstephens and Lily called in at the Star earlier in the day to settle their account.

At 11.45pm Lily Mountstephens kissed her husband good-night and went to bed. Thomas stepped outside to take in the night air. From his doorstep up on the northern side of the valley he could look down across the basin and the thickening lake of mist to see the rear of Commerce Place. From his vantage point he could see the yellow glow from the cellar window where the lights of Star Stores still burned. Arriving home shortly before midnight and joining his landlord to observe the lights on at the Star, Impey commented on the lateness of the hour and the lights still burning at the shop. He suggested that he and Mountstephens walk back across the valley to ensure that all was well with the shopkeeper. Mountstephens shrugged off Impey's concern and described an earlier visit to the store and a conversation with Mr Thomas regarding the latter's intention to remain there after hours. The two men went inside and Mountstephens pointed Impey to the hot supper Lily had left simmering for him. He reminded Impey to be sure to leave enough for the returning Mr Thomas.

At 1am, the shopkeeper had still not returned and Arthur Impey began to fret. The lights at the rear of the Star were still burning. It seemed to Impey odd that a man of Mr Thomas' strict beliefs should still be working well into the Sabbath. He again asked Mountstephens to accompany him across the valley. Again, Mountstephens dismissed his concerns, reminded him of Mr Thomas' warning and went to bed. At 4am, Impey finally gave up waiting for his bed-mate and retired for the night. He wondered whether his landlord might have misunderstood the shopkeeper earlier and perhaps Mr Thomas had arranged to go to Swansea to spend the day of rest with his brother and in his haste forgotten to turn off the lights. Impey, though, was forced to admit he had never known Mr Thomas to take such a course before.

Shortly before 11pm on Saturday, February 12, Priscilla Davies was in the kitchen when her attention was caught by a flickering light at the rear of the row of properties known as Lamb Buildings. Like the rest of Garnant, she was completely unaware of the dramas which had unfolded a few minutes' walk down the road at Star Stores some 45 minutes earlier. She was also unaware of those wondering why the shopkeeper had not returned home for the night. She would remain oblivious to all such matters until the next day. Lamb Buildings, a row of low cottages with a couple of larger buildings at the western end where Upper Station Road joined the valley road, had been built by Priscilla's father William 'The Lamb' Thomas after he had taken out a lease on the plot from Lord Dynevor in 1874. William was one of the men who had helped shape the valley through vision and determination just as, over the years, he had transformed himself from coal miner to property developer to Baptist minister.

The Thomas family were one of Garnant's oldest, with William – who was born in nearby Llandybie on the outskirts of Ammanford in 1833 – setting up home at Nantmain Cottage on the valley road sometime in the early 1850s. Priscilla was born in 1876 – the seventh child of the household. She married builder Thomas Davies in 1909. The couple had a daughter, Hannah, in 1911 while living at Anchor House, the detached property at the end of the row built by her father. Mary Ray had followed in 1915 during the young family's short stay in the nearby town of Pontardawe. By 1921 they had returned to Garnant and were back in one of the Thomas family properties – this time at Lamb House, next door to Anchor House, the building in which Priscilla had been born. Her childhood home was now rented out to paying tenants at 18 shillings a month.

As Priscilla peered out through the window into the darkness of the cold February night she could see the source of the unmistakable flickering light. It came from the rear of Anchor House, where despite the hour and much to her surprise, her neighbours were having a small bonfire. It seemed however that the fire would not last long for, from what Priscilla could make out by the light of the dancing flames, all they been burning was a few old rags. Priscilla considered such activity odd, but thought little more about it. By the time she learned of the drama which had taken place, and with the village alive among rumours of a murder, she had forgotten all about the bonfire in the night.

As the clock neared midnight, Frederick James and fellow members of band began to filter away from Stepney Hall. Frederick, a 31-year-old collier by day and cornet player by night, faced the long walk home to Glanaman along the starry valley road. As he and a band-mate made their way to their beds still buzzing with excitement and energy from a performance, they were surprised to see a lone shop light still burning in the night. The pair moved closer and paused in the arc of gaslight cast from behind the thin blinds of Star Stores.

"Like a spotlight on the stage," Frederick joked.

As their hushed laughter hung in the cold night air, a mischievous grin took shape on Frederick's lips as a thought began to form. He nudged his fellow player closer into the doorway and pulled out a piece of sheet music from his pocket. Holding the paper up against the cold glass of the window so the lights from inside illuminated the notation, Frederick raised his cornet to his lips and, struggling to hold back his giggles, he began to play. His companion raised his own instrument and the pair played out a midnight melody to the otherwise silent valley road. Less than ten feet away – behind the window pane and blinds, the corpse of Thomas Thomas, manager of the Star Supply Stores, was already going cold.

Police Sergeant Thomas Richards and Constable David Thomas walked the valley road beat umpteen times that evening. The Amman Valley derby, played out that afternoon was usually an occasion of boisterous high spirits and drunken brawling as post-match debate raged, but this time there was little to report. The two men were pleased that despite the ill-feeling between the supporters of the warring sides, and the controversy surrounding Ammanford's brutal tactics, there had been no major problems beyond the customary Saturday night drunkenness to keep them from their rounds. Both officers noted that the lights remained on in the Star, where two of the sergeant's children were employed, each time they passed, but saw no reason to investigate. The two officers remained unconcerned when they strolled past the shop on their final patrol at 11pm, although they did attempt to peer in through the window. They, like the little Bowen girl almost an hour earlier, could see nothing untoward through the thin gap between the drawn-down blinds and the window frame. With no reason for alarm, they made their way back to the station, near Raven Colliery to the east of Commerce Place and beyond Lamb Buildings.

Dr George Evan Jones, of Brynteg, also passed the Star a little after 11pm, summoned on a late-night call. He too spotted the gas lights burning inside, but like those before him thought little of it. Besides, he had a far more pressing engagement. At

3am the weary doctor passed along the front of Commerce Place once more as he made for home. He also stopped outside the Star and tried to peer in around the blinds. With no sign of life and nothing but a peaceful silence emanating from inside, he shrugged off whatever doubts he may have had and made, exhausted, for his bed. He would be summoned back to the Star next morning.

Chapter Two:
There is a light and the door is open

MORGAN WALTER JEFFREYS should have had more reasons than most to feel satisfied with his lot in life. Throughout his fifty-eight years, the butcher, grocer, businessman, property developer and landlord had experienced the suffering and hardship that either broke a man or steeled him. Jeffreys had remained unbroken, though now ill health and age coupled with the strife and stress of business were slowly wearing him down. Where he had dreamt of an old age spent in comfort and wealth, two decades in the courts battling one of the most powerful men in Wales had gnawed away at the prosperity others imagined him to boast. Despite his difficulties, his standing in the eyes of others was important to him. He was delighted to be thought of as a wealthy, successful man. He knew the importance of image. Even within the four walls of his home he refused to show his weaknesses and he did his best to hide from his wife Anne the the worsening headaches which now struck him with a growing regularity.

He had been born into the relative prosperity that came with land ownership, but had watched helplessly as it all but disappeared before he could reach an age to put it to good use. His father, also named Morgan, had inherited 250 acres, and employed six farmhands, a housemaid, a general servant, a nurse and a groom by the time his second son arrived in 1862. Morgan senior had been handed control of Ystradwalter, the family farm near Llandovery, at the age of fifty following the death of his parents who passed away within months of each other in the spring of 1855. Only then, with land and assets finally to his name, had Morgan taken a wife. He married Mary Williams, a woman thirteen years his junior, in the warm summer of 1856. His first-born, David, arrived in 1859. Three years later, Morgan junior was delivered safe and well, but his father was already 62 years of age and would not live to celebrate his second son's sixth birthday.

With two young sons to care for and widowed on the cusp of her fiftieth birthday, Mary had no desire to maintain the family farm. It was not her business after all and she was no farmer, having craved only a life of ease and comfort. She sold Ystradwalter to the highest bidder at the earliest opportunity and moved her family lock, stock and barrel into the nearby bustling market town on the banks of the rolling River Towy. In so doing, she turned her back on the land which had prospered under the Jeffreys family name for generations and had been the bedrock on which they had built their impressive reputation. The money from the sale ensured Mary would never need worry or toil again, but without the income generated from the land, and the crops and livestock it hosted, her sons would be forced to find their own way through life. By his early teens Morgan junior had already left the safety of the family home and turned his back on farming once and for all. He travelled the 36 miles across the Brecon Beacons to take up a post a grocer's assistant in the mining town of Aberdare where, under the wing of another Llandovery exile – a man named Rees Davies – he learned the skills required of a shopkeeper.

His ambition ensured he would not be content to remain anyone's assistant for long, and by his mid-twenties, Morgan Jeffreys was a married man with an assistant of his own and a thriving business in Roath, a bustling working-class district of Cardiff. The town was still decades from earning city status or becoming the Welsh capital, but nevertheless it was growing faster than anywhere else in the principality as relentless coal, iron and copper shipments poured through its docks and made it rich. Within a decade and before the century had turned, Jeffreys had sold his burgeoning business, returning west with his young family in tow. He bought the property Glanynant just off the valley road in Garnant and once again set up his own grocer's shop, this time expanding his market with the skills he had learned in Cardiff and proclaiming himself a butcher. Morgan had timed his arrival to perfection – Garnant and neighbouring Glanaman were booming as the coal mines and tinworks swelled the villages with incomers. He was a man who understood that where there were workers with money in their pockets there was profit to be had. Communities such as Garnant needed men like Morgan Jeffreys – men of vision, ambition and drive.

In 1895, he – or rather his wife Anne – had leased the land alongside the valley road adjoining Glanynant from Lord Dynevor with the intention of building an empire. The deal was not all they had imagined and the disputes that followed saw them embroiled in the twenty year legal row with the Dynevor Estate which would almost break them. In 1903, the title deeds for the land were transferred from Anne to Morgan and in 1911 were transferred again – this time into the name of Morgan Walter Williams-Jeffreys, though why Morgan choose to incorporate his mother's maiden name with his father's surname to become a double-barrelled landowner remains a mystery – there appears no other time on record when the title was used – apart from his death certificate.

The legal wranglings between the Jeffreys and Lord Dynevor centred on the requirement to improve the road outside the properties – and the responsibility for meeting the inevitable costs. Between 1895 and 1915, the Jeffreys refused to pay a penny in ground-rent, claiming the Estate had responsibility for the road. Lord Dynevor saw things differently. The row culminated in a High Court appearance and an order that Morgan and Anne pay £74, 13s. 7½d in back rent. The order in itself was not a massive bill, but the courtroom battle all but bankrupted the couple.

"Both Mr and Mrs Jeffreys are impecunious people," Lord Dynevor's solicitor warned his employer in a letter of 1913. They were penniless, at least as far as the lawyers could tell. Somehow however, with the legal fight finally lost, they funded the building of Commerce Place during the war years – initially six shops with storage or living accommodation above. The couple had plans to construct another six in what would become Coronation Arcade, and, over time, their vision became reality. They renamed Glanynant – their home – Commerce House in keeping with their elevated position and it seemed, at least to those looking on, sat back to count their rental income. In reality the properties barely covered the cost of maintaining their debts and much like in the days of Morgan's own youth, his sons, who might have expected some degree of luxury in their lives, were sent out to work. In the Amman Valley work meant heading underground and whatever the standing of their father, the Jeffreys boys were forced to join their neighbours at the coalface.

Morgan always liked to start his day with a cup of tea. On any normal Sunday Anne would have attended to such domestic chores and Morgan would already have been seated in his favourite chair in front of the fire, his pipe lit and the morning papers spread across the kitchen table. On February 12, 1921, however his wife of thirty-one years and more twists and turns than he dared recall, was unwell. She had seemed fine the previous evening though in truth he had gone from pub to ponies to bed and given her little chance to tell him that she was coming down with a cold. When they had woken at 8.30am, Anne's condition had deteriorated and she remained in her bed for most of the day. With Morgan faced with fending for himself for once, the 58-year-old got up and set about lighting the fire and stove in a bid to bring some much-needed warmth to the house on a cold, crisp winter morning. It was only then that he realised there was not a drop of milk in the house. Fortunately, Morgan – his eldest son – was already up, despite nursing the after-effects of spending his Saturday night – and most of his weekly wage – drinking in Ammanford, Glanaman and Garnant. With little consideration for his fragile condition, the 28-year-old was despatched to the nearby farm with an empty jug in his hand. Morgan Powell Jeffreys had been gone barely long enough to hop over the low wall between the Jeffreys' home and the neighbouring Star Stores before he returned. Morgan senior was at the cold-water tap filling the kettle when his son reappeared in the doorway."There is a light at the Star, and the door is open," he told his father.

The time was approaching 9am. The head of the household paused a moment as the copper kettle in his hands grew heavier. The rear door to the Star opened into a cellar. A staircase ran from the dark, damp storage area up to the back room, which in turn opened out into the shop at street level.

"Oh, Mr Thomas is sure to be there," he said after giving the matter some thought. "Call out to him."

Morgan nodded and climbed the wall once more before approaching the rear of the shop. At the open back door he stopped and called to the shopkeeper. He returned to the house to report that he had received no response, though whether he shouted loud enough for Thomas Thomas, stone deaf in one ear and partially deaf in the other, to have heard seems unlikely. He suggested that his father rouse Miss Jones, the head assistant at the Star who lodged with the family, before climbing the wall once more and making his way across the field towards the farm. Morgan junior, with his mouth parched and the previous day's drinking pounding on his brain, was far more interested in a cup of tea than the comings and goings of shopkeepers.

Morgan senior, meanwhile, considered the implications of what his son had said. He recalled having seen that the gas lights were still burning the previous evening when he had gone to bed the ponies and now they were lit still, illuminating the inside of shop the following morning. The fact that the cellar door was open only served to complicate matters further. He wondered whether the door might have been open when he passed the previous night. Strangely, he would initially tell the *Amman Valley Chronicle* reporter that it had been he who first spotted the lights at the Star and noticed that the door was open, however in the space of a week or two his version of events would slowly evolve to be more in keeping with the recollections of his son. Whether it was Morgan senior or junior who first spotted that the door was ajar, it is certainly true that the elder man eventually decided to take his son's advice and it was he who called up to Miss Jones, though he thought it best to deal with such matters as delicately as he could.

In a bid not to startle or frighten the young lady, he decided he would avoid alerting her to the events at her place of work immediately. Instead, he chose to call up the stairs to ask whether she would be attending chapel that morning. In her room upstairs, Phoebe Jones was annoyed to be disturbed so early on her one day off. Her annoyance was exacerbated by the strangeness of the question. Mr Jeffreys knew all too well that Phoebe was not a regular chapel-goer. The thought of some Hell and damnation preacher sentencing her to the fire and brimstone for her sins in a freezing chapel as she failed abysmally to make herself comfortable on a granite-hard pew held little appeal compared to the warmth of her bed on a Sunday morning. The Bible-quoting Mr Thomas, her employer, provided enough parables and lessons from the Good Book for her during the working week. She saw no need to subject herself to additional condemnation. It was therefore with only thinly-veiled irritation in her voice that she shouted back down the stairs that she had no intention of visiting the chapel.

Ten minutes later, Mr Jeffreys called up to her again. On the second occasion however, he informed her that the rear door of the Star was open and the lights were on. Phoebe was more than willing to take her chances in the judgement of the Almighty if it gained her another hour beneath the blankets, but her position as first assistant at the Star was a far more pressing, corporeal concern. She knew immediately that all was not well. She leapt from her bed and dressed as quickly as she was able. Within a matter of minutes she was in the kitchen where the kettle was beginning to boil. When she went out of the back door of the house she saw Mr Jeffreys standing at the rear of the Star, poking his head in the open cellar door and calling out to Mr Thomas. His pleas came and went without response. Morgan junior was returning with a jug of warm milk as Miss Jones made her way up the path to the rear door of the shop. He sat down on the wall between the Star and his home with an air of curious indifference as his father appraised Miss Jones of the situation. Tentatively, Phoebe pushed open the rear door of the Star and like the two Jeffreys men before her, called out to Mr Thomas. She too was met with silence. With the determined resolve of a woman making her own way in life, she stepped into the cellar and began to climb the steps leading up into the back room. As she stepped up onto the first of the stairs, her head drew level with the floor of the rear room where the safe was located and which in turn led through the open doorway into the shop itself. The sight which met her set her heart pumping her chest. The safe door was wide open and its contents were scattered around the room. Drawers were half-pulled open as if they had been hurriedly searched. Insurance cards were spread over the floor, as were some of the dusters and cleaning swabs which were kept in the safe. The two tin boxes in which the day's takings were placed before being locked away for the night were lying on the floor as if thrown down. The tins were open and clearly empty. She took another step on the stairs, and then another. When she placed her foot on the third step she was able to see through the open doorway into the interior of the shop itself. The vision which met her would remain in her nightmares for the rest of her life.

Thomas Thomas was lying on his back behind the provisions counter. His booted feet were nearest to her as the shopkeeper lay stretched into the shop's interior, but from her position on the stairs and the position of the body she could see his face, turned at some strange angle to meet her gaze, was smeared with blood. A thick red pool had congealed on the floor around where he lay. His eyes were open and his mouth hung in a fiendish gape. As the scream burst from Phoebe's lips, she looked into the eyes of Thomas Thomas and the dead man stared back. Phoebe screamed his name, but she knew that Thomas Thomas was already in the arms of the Almighty.

Morgan Walter Jeffreys was barely a step behind her when Phoebe Jones gave out her awful scream. It was the second such pitiful howl to have been heard within the walls of the Star Supply Stores in a matter of hours. Miss Jones froze stock still for a moment as if the horror she faced had drained her of momentum and Mr Jeffreys was forced into an evasive manoeuvre to avoid crashing into the back of the young woman and knocking her flat on her face.

"Mr Thomas!" she shrieked.

There was nothing but silence. After a heartbeat pause that seemed to last an hour, Phoebe spun on her heels and in a state of great distress bustled her way past Mr Jeffreys. She raced down the steps and out of the cellar door before her landlord had time to catch his breath. Within seconds of Phoebe disappearing out into the morning sunshine, Morgan junior burst in with a look of bewildered panic on his face. Mr Jeffreys turned and, followed by his son, slowly took another step upwards. As his eye-level rose above that of the top step he too caught sight of the vision that had so terrified Phoebe.

Thomas Thomas, the shopkeeper, lay dead behind the provisions counter, head towards the front windows. One leg stretched back towards the rear of the shop, and pushed out of the doorway into the back room closest to Morgan Jeffreys. The other was bent at the knee against a box on the floor. The dead man lay on his back, but his head was slightly turned so, with eyes wide open, he looked directly into the eyes of those coming up the stairs. He head had been bashed open and a pool of blood had congealed around him. His shirt front was soaked and his neck and collar were stained dark red. A box nearby was also splashed with that vital fluid. The safe was wide open and papers and cards and various other items were scattered about the back room floor. Both men, like Phoebe before them, took a moment to comprehend the sight that met them before they too were sent reeling backwards down the stair and out into the sharp morning air.

The sound of the father and son bursting out of the rear door of the Star Stores startled William Copestake, another tenant of Morgan Jeffreys. Copestake lived with his wife in rooms above one of the shops in Coronation Arcade. He had stepped outside to collect some coal for the fire just a moment after Phoebe Jones had burst from the store and raced back into Commerce House and was unaware of the shop assistant's distress, but saw the two Jeffreys men stumble back into the sunlight. Copestake originally hailed from Derbyshire and was another who had made his way to South Wales in search of work. He had arrived in the Amman Valley around 1896, aged 20. It was not long before he made the acquaintance of Margaret Davies, a woman almost twice his age. They married in the summer of 1897 and their first child, a daughter named Mary, duly arrived some five months later. By 1901, Copestake was underground hewing coal, just as his father had done in the pits of Derbyshire. The work was hard and life was a struggle. William was not destined to spend long underground however having fled from the north of England to escape such backbreaking toil. By 1911 he had willingly accepted a lesser wage to work as a farmhand in the employ of Sarah Hicks at Waunwhiad Farm in Glanaman. A reduction in his earnings to avoid the graft of mining may have been acceptable to Copestake, but his family had suffered. While he had found bed and board with the widow Hicks in exchange for sweat and labour, his family was not so fortunate. Margaret, now in her mid fifties, along with Mary, and their other children William junior and Annie were destined to become residents of the Llandeilo Union Workhouse. But by the time the two Jeffreys men burst pale-faced and gasping into the sunlight through the rear cellar door of the Star on that chill February morning, Copestake was aged 45 – Margaret was 60. Despite their past woes the couple were now in residence in rooms above the Arcade. William called over to the two men in greeting – it was always good to remain on friendly terms with one's landlord – but he was made immediately aware that something was seriously wrong. Mr Jeffreys called him over and told him of the horrors inside the store. The three men returned inside and climbed the steps to where William Copestake became the fourth person to look upon the body of the shopkeeper lying lifeless behind his counter. The three men quickly decided on their next course of action. Copestake was dispatched to fetch the doctor. Morgan Jeffreys junior was sent to summon the police. Meanwhile, two young boys from the village who wandered over having had their attentions drawn by the commotion were sent by Mr Jeffreys to fetch Mr Mountstephens from Glanyrafon Villas with a message that he must come at once. Morgan Jeffreys senior would remain at the scene of the crime.

Chapter Three:
You must come at once

SERGEANT THOMAS RICHARDS was leaning on the counter of Garnant Police Station filling out the station diary which he completed diligently each morning, noting an unremarkable night in the village, when Morgan Jeffreys burst through the door. Richards had joined the constabulary in January 1895 at the age of twenty-one and had been stationed in various towns around the county before transferring to Garnant in May 1913, a month after his promotion, which had been earned while stationed in the village of Ferryside, some 25 miles to the west. The village police station was also home to Sergeant Richards and his wife Mary Ann along with their children Maggie, Hubert, Nellie, Emlyn and Gwyneth as well PC Thomas and his family.

Richards was no great fan of Morgan Powell Jeffreys and had had an eye on the 28-year-old miner for some time. A quarter century of policing had taught him who he was able to trust and honed his natural instinct to identify those likely to be the troublemaker in the pack. Morgan Powel Jeffreys had a well-earned reputation as a drinker – and a man who committed the various sins and misdemeanours that all too often walked hand in hand with a love of the bottle. However it did not take an experienced officer such as Thomas Richards to recognise that something was seriously wrong. It was clear that the breathless Jeffreys had run the entire distance from Commerce Place to the station more than half a mile east along the valley road.

"You must come to the Star shop at once," pleaded Jeffreys, before he was even fully through the door.

The sergeant could smell stale beer and whisky, but to see a man like Jeffreys, a man who had experienced the horrors of the Great War, in such distress was an alarming sight.

"Mr Thomas, the manager is lying behind the provisions

counter. His head must have been bashed in, as he was lying in a pool of blood."

The policeman's pocket-watch said 9.25am. He summoned his only constable, John Thomas, and the pair set off behind Morgan Jeffreys to the open rear door of the Star. Like those who had come before him, the first thing Sergeant Richards noted as he climbed the stairs from the basement back door of the Star Stores to the ground floor rear storeroom was that the safe was open and there was paperwork, invoices and receipts, scattered around the floor. As he looked further through the open doorway into the rear of the shop, he saw the body of Thomas Thomas. There was no doubt in the policeman's mind that Thomas Thomas was dead. His experience and profession-alism immediately clicked into action and he ordered PC Thomas to secure the premises while he went to examine the body.

The shopkeeper's blank eyes watched the policeman as he climbed the steps into the store room. The arms lay partly on the body. The right leg was straight, the left leg, partly bent. There was a deep gash on the left-hand side of the shopkeeper's throat and blood had pooled on the floor around him and stained the collar of his clothing. Another deep wound scarred his right temple and there were also cuts and bruises to his left ear. One of his eyes was discoloured and there was an open wound on his cheek. The upper part of the dead man's trousers, the lower part of his waistcoat and a portion of his cardigan jacket were open. Richards could see that the waistcoat, shirt and vest had been deliberately drawn up while the trousers had been unbuttoned and pulled down to expose the abdomen. The clothing was stained dark red. Lying close to the body – some three or four inches from the left shoulder – was the upper set of a pair of dentures embedded in a block of cheese. The lower set of teeth lay some six inches away from the dead man's left knee. A brass brush-head was also on the floor, about six inches beyond the top of Thomas Thomas' head. Thick red blood was congealing in its bristles. There were bloody marks on a wooden margarine case a little to the right of the head. The shop itself appeared in perfect order, save for the corpse on the floor. Everything else appeared in orderly condition and seemed to have been undisturbed.

Dr George Evan Jones, having been pulled from his late breakfast by William Copestake, arrived at Star Stores only moments behind Sergeant Richards and PC Thomas. The doctor, who ran a successful practice in the village and was considered the foremost physician in the valley, immediately set about the task of carrying out an initial, albeit brief, medical examination of the corpse. He pronounced Thomas Thomas deceased at 9.45am. During the course of his inspection, the doctor noted that the shopkeeper's left wrist and hand were covered with blood, but that there was no blood at all on the palms and none on the right hand. The head was pressed up against a box on his right and lying in a pool of blood. The front of the margarine case was splattered with blood. There was bruising and minor injuries to the right side of the face and temple as well as bruising to the left temple and eye. On the right side of the head, two incisions cut to the bone. The neck had been punctured in the region of the carotid sheath. The trousers were unbuttoned except the two last lower buttons. The pants were unbuttoned, and the waistcoat undone at the lower button. The front of the shirt and vest were raised up, as was the cardigan. The clothing was soaked with blood, but appeared on preliminary examination to be otherwise undamaged. A lump of cheese was firmly impressed in the palate of the artificial teeth of the upper jaw. It was the doctor's view that Thomas Thomas had died approximately eleven hours earlier – between 10pm and 11pm the previous night.

While Dr Jones carried out his examination of the body, PS Richards and PC Thomas began a search of the premises. Close to the skull of the deceased was the head of a broom, the bristles of which were smeared with congealed blood. The handle which should have been attached to the broomhead was nowhere to be seen. On the grocery counter, which ran along the left-hand side of the shop as customers entered from the door onto the valley road, a cash book lay open. From what the sergeant could tell there appeared to be a number of incomplete entries. Next to the book was a provisions stock sheet and a registered envelope addressed to the Star Tea Company, 292-314 Old Street, London, E.C. Inside the envelope was a set of till rolls. Also on the grocery counter was a small canvas bag containing five shillings and two pence. The nearby till was open and there was two shillings worth of bronze in the tray. There was another three shillings in bronze in the till on the provisions counter, which was also open. The rest of the shop was in perfect order, and everything seemed to have been left undisturbed. In the store-room to the rear where the safe had been left open, were the two empty tin boxes, open and laying on their sides on the floor as if thrown down or tossed aside. Insurance cards, invoices, shop and company paperwork and various items of business correspondence was scattered around the room. Dusters and cleaning rags also lay about the place. The safe drawers were pulled open. A ring of keys hung from the safe key which was still in the lock.

Leaning against the wall at the foot of the stairs leading from the cellar to the warehouse, PC Thomas found the iron bar which was used to form part of the back door's locking system. The bar was smeared in blood. While Richards searched the premises for fingerprints, PC Thomas went outside to look for footprints or other clues as to movements at the rear of the shop. There was little to find however, with night temperatures falling well below freezing the ground had proved too firm to catch any distinct impressions. There was nothing else which could be deemed a clue. Richards was slightly more fortunate inside the building and a number of sets of fingerprints, albeit faint and indistinct, were identified. There were two relatively clear impressions on the provision counter butter block, close to where the body had fallen. There was also a number of finger-marks on a lower shelf behind the counter. All the impressions were marked and secured by Sergeant Richards in preparation for recording.

As Richards and Thomas continued their respective searches, Thomas Mountstephens arrived at the shop in a state of panic. Deputy Chief Constable John Evans arrived shortly after from Llandeilo having been telephoned by Sergeant Richards' wife from Garnant station, and he was followed by the Chief Constable of the Carmarthenshire Constabulary, William Picton Phillipps and uniformed officers from Carmarthen. Each arrival was appraised of the situation by Sergeant Richards while Mountstephens was forced to tell and retell the story of the shopkeeper's failure to return home as expected the previous evening. Once the senior men were satisfied, the body of Thomas Thomas was carried to a hearse which had been summoned by Deputy Chief Constable Evans and removed to his lodgings across the valley at Glanyrafon Villas. A crowd of onlookers had already begun to gather in the street outside the shop when the body was loaded into the vehicle. Mountstephens meanwhile was instructed to take his motor car to Swansea to collect the brother of the dead man who would be informed – by telephone – of the tragedy by the Chief Constable himself. The remaining officers, marshalled by Deputy Chief Constable Evans, then secured the scene both inside and out to prevent any interference with articles which might be deemed to offer any clue.

Chapter Four:
A most harmless man

ON THE MORNING OF MONDAY, February 14, Dr George Evan Jones, assisted by the junior partner at his practice, Trefor Hughes Rhys, began the gruesome task of carrying out a post-mortem examination on the body of the shopkeeper. Jones was a North Walian by birth though his mother's family hailed from Cheshire. He had been sent to his mother's home county for his education before undergoing medical training at Edinburgh University, where he was a contemporary of Arthur Conan Doyle, creator of the world famous detective Sherlock Holmes. No doubt Dr Jones was keen to prove his own worth in the field of forensic medicine and show himself as useful to the real police as his class-mate had been to his imagined sleuth on the pages of *Strand* magazine. Rhys meanwhile hailed originally from Kidwelly some 30 miles east of Garnant on the River Gwendraeth. Like Conan Doyle's own medical creation and right-hand man to the great detective, Dr Rhys had used his skills as surgeon on the battlefield. He earned the rank of Captain in the Royal Army Medical Corps during the Great War, and saw more than his share of bloodshed and death in Mesopotamia in the spring of 1918. After the war, Rhys came home to Wales and the fiancée he had left behind. He married his childhood sweetheart Dora in Pembroke in the spring of 1920 and the young couple immediately moved to the Amman Valley and a new life where the now 30-year-old Rhys took up the vacancy alongside Dr Jones.

The two men set about the examination with a grim stoicism. Both had experienced the worst injuries suffered by man, whether from the battlefield or the pit, but the mutilated body of the frail shopkeeper bore witness to a unique tragedy. Upon removing the scalp, the medics – with Dr Jones taking the lead – immediately noted a fracture of the squamous portion of the temporal bone on the right-hand side of the skull around the area occupied by the ear. There were also fractures to parts of the front and right parietal bone on the upper part of the skull which were now in contact with the temporal bone. A total of eleven separate pieces of bone had been broken from the main bones and were pressing on the membranous coverings and onto the brain itself. The zygomatic bone – the cheek bone – was also fractured in two places. On the right side of the neck was a puncture wound. The doctors traced the trajectory of the wound and found it to pass upwards and inwards, just missing the carotid sheath before passing underneath the floor of the mouth, cutting through the root of the tongue, slicing through the left tonsil and almost passing out on the left side of the neck. There was a deep puncture wound in the abdomen just below the lower end of the sternum, the central bone of the chest to which the ribs attach. Dr Jones traced the wound, which passed through the left lobe of the liver and along the small curvature of the stomach, leaving a slight incision into the stomach, and then through the left kidney. The stomach was practically empty with the exception of some fluid and a small piece of partially digested meat. There was no trace of any cheese in the stomach or digestive system. All the internal organs were healthy but pale due to the considerable loss of blood. The doctors agreed to formally record that Thomas Thomas had died between 9pm and midnight on Saturday, February 12.

When Diana Bowen, the only adult who might be considered a witness to the murder of Thomas Thomas, told police she heard "an awful screech as of a boy or some weak person" from inside Star Stores she was without doubt describing the final moments of the shopkeeper. In a community where men earned their living either at the coal-face or within touching distance of the red-hot furnaces of the tin-plate works, where life was cheap and death only a single slip or error of judgement away, Thomas Thomas was a weak person. He was forty-four years of age when he died and had spent his entire working life behind a shop counter. Compared to the men who made up the population of Cwmaman, Thomas Thomas was indeed a weak and sickly man. He was frail and had battled ill-health his entire life. He was of poor physique, afflicted by deafness, most particularly in the left ear but also in his right, which had shown gradual deterioration as he aged. An accident in childhood had left him with a deformity of the right leg which caused him to limp and affected his balance. A week before his murder, he had undergone surgery for a nasal complaint at a Swansea clinic.

"He was never very robust," his brother would later say. "He suffered from headaches and varicose veins. He was almost stone deaf in one ear and this had affected the other."

According to those that knew him, though the indication appears to be that few in Garnant knew him well, he was a man of regular and simple habits and, according to his landlord, "of a studious nature".

"He was a most harmless man," Thomas Mountstephens would say. "He had not an enemy in the world".

A bachelor, Thomas was also devout in his worship and in his clothing was found a number of newspaper cuttings relating to religion and spiritualism which he appeared to have turned to in his darkest hours. They were worn and well-thumbed and had clearly been read repeatedly. He took on management of the Garnant branch of Star Stores in November 1919 having previously been employed, according to his brother John, "in similar positions" for 15 years at branches of the Star in Bridgend and Llandeilo. It is likely that Thomas spent his entire working life in the employment of the Star Tea Company, owners of the Star Stores chain of shops. He was born in 1877 in the village of Llangendeirne – Llangyndeyrn in its pure Welsh form – to James and Elizabeth Thomas. Llangendeirne lies some 20 miles directly west of Garnant. James was a well-known local shoemaker who was born and lived his entire life in Llangendeirne. Elizabeth was also born and raised in the village. Thomas was the eldest of the couple's three children and was arrived when both his parents had reached the age of 37. By the age of fourteen, he had left the family home and was a paying lodger at 38 King St, Carmarthen, where he worked as a shopkeeper's apprentice. There was certainly a Star Stores in Carmarthen at this time though whether Thomas was then employed by the company is not known. At some point during the next decade he left rural Carmarthenshire and moved to Cardiff, just as Morgan Jeffreys had done a decade before. By

1901 Thomas was employed as a shop assistant while boarding at 11 Stockland Street in the Canton district of Cardiff. Again, the Star Tea Company certainly had a store in the town, though whether Thomas was an employee remains uncertain. He may have moved to Cardiff in search of more than was on offer in Carmarthenshire, but it does certainly seem a distinct possibility that he was moving from one branch of the Star to another.

By 1911, Thomas was branch manager of the Bridgend and Maesteg branch of Star Stores, renting a room – or at least a bed – at Y Gongl, 12 Port Terrace, Maesteg. Precisely how long he remained in Maesteg – or Bridgend if his brother's comments are correct – is unknown, but at some point between 1911 and 1918 he had moved again to take over the management of the Llandeilo branch of the chain, before then replacing the outgoing manager at Garnant in 1919. Thomas was only the second branch manager at Garnant – the store having opened for the first time around 1916 in the new buildings erected as part of Morgan Jeffreys Commerce Place development. Upon arrival in Garnant, Thomas took over not only the job of his predecessor but also his lodgings at Two Glanyrafon Villas.

While the doctors set about their grisly task over the River Amman and across the rugby field at Glanyrafon Villas, Deputy Chief Constable Evans oversaw the beginnings of the investigation within the walls of Star Stores. Phoebe Jones, was summoned and was instructed to carry out a brief inventory of the store to assess whether any items were missing or had been disturbed. When she satisfied herself that the shop was as it should be, she was asked to inspect the storeroom area. The warehouse was strewn with paper and items from the safe, but she could see nothing missing apart from the money which should have been in the two empty tins. After a pause however, she looked again. A boning knife, usually kept in the safe, was also missing. There were seven knives in all used in the shop, but only six could now be located. The knife had a red handle and Phoebe herself had used it a number of times on Saturday. The broom used to brush the shop floor which was kept against the wall next to the safe was also missing. The broomhead was identical in all aspects to the one on the floor behind the provisions counter and Phoebe was in no doubt they were one and the same; the handle was nowhere to be seen. She was also asked to examine the day's receipts and calculate the amount of money missing.

Meanwhile, Sergeant Richards summoned his fourteen-year-old son Emlyn and Trevor Morgan, the second of the Star's young errand boys and general assistants. Emlyn had left school the previous year and had been lucky to gain a position alongside his elder sister Nellie as an assistant at the Star. At thirteen, Trevor Morgan was in his final year of school and worked at the Star after classes and on Saturdays. The boys were set the task of searching the fields to the rear of the Star up to the River Amman. Anything unusual was to remain untouched and be reported back PC Thomas immediately. At 10.45am, the pair raced out-of-breath up the hill back to the rear of the shop where the PC Thomas was examining the garden area behind the row of shops and the Jeffreys' home at Commerce House.

Some 200 yards to the rear of the back gardens of the houses in the little stream – or nant – which ran down the valley side to join the River Amman and which had given the village its name, the boys discovered a broken broom handle. It was submerged and had been pinned to the bottom of the brook by heavy stones. Constable Thomas carefully retrieved the broom handle before he and the boys scoured the remainder of the small stream, starting at the top and working their way back down to the river. They found a knife wedged beneath a large stone in the deepest part of the stream no more than a dozen yards further downstream from where the broom handle had been hidden. The blade was speckled with rust and bloodstains. Its handle was dark brown. Thomas summoned those constables from Llandeilo and Carmarthen who had remained in Garnant overnight and a thorough search was carried out of the field, particularly around the brook, and also the hedges, gateways and muddy areas in the hope that a set of footprints or some other evidence might be discovered, but nothing more was found. Meanwhile at Number Two Glanyrafon Villas, the dead man's clothes were examined. Despite the stab wounds to Thomas Thomas' body, his clothing – though stained with blood – was undamaged. In his pockets was £15 and a penny in cash, along with his pocket watch and the religious newspaper cuttings.

At the Star Stores, Phoebe Jones had double-checked the receipts. They represented, she told Deputy Chief Constable Evans, the takings from Friday and Saturday. Mr Thomas had last been to the bank on Thursday. There was £128 and two-and-a-half pence missing. There was now no doubt that the murder has been committed during a robbery. Immediately, Deputy Chief Constable Evans relayed the information to the Chief Constable. William Picton Phillipps in turn contacted Llandeilo Post Office with instructions that a telegram be sent in all haste. The telegram, despatched at 12.20pm, was addressed to Handcuffs, London, the address used to send a message to New Scotland Yard, the home of the Metropolitan Police and the Criminal Investigation Department. The department was the base for the elite detectives charged with investigating all murders committed on the UK mainland. The telegram read: "Murder committed Garnant Carmarthenshire Saturday night or yesterday morning early sometime. Send an officer to assist."

The message was signed: Chief Constable of Carmarthenshire. Llandeilo Station, but came with a short postscript: "Officer should proceed to police station, Garnant."

The telegram – number 123969 – was transmitted to Parliament Square Post Office and from there was hand-delivered to the desk sergeant at New Scotland Yard, arriving just over three-quarters of an hour after it was sent from Llandeilo, at 1.06pm.

With Sergeant Richards attending the post-mortem examination at the dead man's lodgings, and Phoebe Jones' inventory of the shop complete, PC Thomas was left alone on the premises with the relatively straightforward task of securing the Star Stores from prying eyes and probing fingers. The task was to prove far more problematic than expected however. News of the crime had spread through the Amman Valley faster than a firedamp explosion underground and crowds had begun gathering outside the shop immediately after rumours of the murder started to emerge. All day Sunday and throughout Monday morning ghoulish sightseers gossiped along the valley road, exchanging titbits of information and speculation while attempting to peer past the drawn shades of the Star's front windows. PC Thomas had been left with strict instructions to ensure that none gained entry to the shop and with the lesser, more optimistic task of encouraging those gathered outside to disperse. While the two doctors were cleaning the wounds of Thomas Thomas less than a mile from the scene of his grisly end, a determined knock at the front door of the Star drew PC Thomas' attention from the darkening pools of congealed blood behind the provisions counter. He opened the front door a little to see the crowd had pulled back, allowing a small gathering of formidable-looking elderly women to make their way to the door. The deputation, armed with buckets, mops, rags and brushes, was led by a number of the village matriarchs, women grown strong and determined by brutal lives spent dealing with husbands and sons hardened by long days underground and loud evenings in the pub. Faced with such a fearsome mob of housewives, PC Thomas' protestations bore little likelihood of success. While the men of Garnant defined their lives down the pit, on the sports pitch or in the pub, the women were governed by far higher powers. Each Sunday, the many chapels of the Amman Valley were filled with the faithful while ministers preached Hell and damnation from the pulpits. PC Thomas was told in no uncertain terms that for the blood of Thomas Thomas to have been left on the floorboards of Star Stores was ungodly, unchristian and quite simply unacceptable. The authority of the Carmarthenshire Constabulary and even the officers of New Scotland Yard paled into insignificance compared to that of the Almighty.

To the woman of the Garnant, every drop of blood on the floor of Number Two, Commerce Place, was blasphemy and an abomination to the eyes of God. Faced by the laws of the Good Book and women who feared the policeman's uniform no more than they did the fist of a tired, drunken husband, PC David Thomas was powerless. His arguments were dismissed and he found himself pushed aside as the women streamed in. Galvinised metal mop buckets clanked and screeched as they were laid out and pushed, with soapsuds overflowing, around the Star as the women set about their pious chores. PC Thomas sent word to Sergeant Richards to come at once, but he knew his effort would be in vain – by the time his senior officer received the call and returned to the shop, the last of Thomas Thomas' blood and all evidence of the gruesome crime which had occurred there would be gone.

Two hours after the arrival of Chief Constable Picton Phillipps' telegram at Scotland Yard, a meeting was already underway in the Commissioner's Office of the Criminal Investigation Department at the headquarters of the Metropolitan Police Force. One of those present was Divisional Detective Inspector George Robert Nicholls. Nicholls was a month shy of his forty-fourth birthday and had twenty-three years service with the Met under his belt, twenty-one of which as a detective with the Criminal Investigation Department. A brown-haired, blue-eyed Londoner standing five-foot-ten in his stocking feet, Nicholls was the quintessential Metropolitan Police officer. The married father of two had been selected from the available senior officers to travel to West Wales and lead the investigation into the killing of Thomas Thomas at the Star Stores.

Enquiries were made and tickets booked from London to Cardiff where they would change trains and move on to Llanelli in Carmarthenshire. There a coal wagon would – after unloading its cargo of Amman Valley anthracite – await their arrival and carry them north to the shellshocked village of Garnant. With the details agreed, Nicholls telephoned the Chief Constable of the Carmarthenshire Constabulary to confirm that he and his sergeant could be expected to arrive shortly after first light the following morning.

PART TWO

Chapter Five:
The huntsman and the shooting star

AS THE COAL TRAIN approached the station at Garnant in the murky pre-dawn hours, Nicholls' arrival echoed that of another huntsman from a tale well-known to the residents of Cwmaman. Nicholls had been summoned by the Chief Constable of Carmarthenshire to hunt the killer of a shopkeeper; King Arthur had been called upon to pursue his own murderous quarry throughout the Valley. In the story of Culhwch and Olwen, the ancient tale which forms part of the *Mabinogion*, Arthur is despatched to Cwmaman to chase the mythic Twrch Trwyth, whom God had transformed into a giant boar as punishment for his sins. Nicholls could only hope that his target would prove so easy to identify. While Arthur had selected a band of his finest knights to accompany him, the detective – for his quest – had chosen just one. Detective Sergeant Charles Canning was of similar stature to Nicholls and was only six months younger than his senior officer. He had joined the Met in 1902 and had spent his career stationed at Marylebone and Greenwich before transferring to the CID Commissioner's Office in December 1918. He was a man who enjoyed Nicholls trust, respect and friendship. As with the band of brothers who pursued the boar along the banks of the River Amman in a time beyond reckoning, so too did Nicholls and Canning reach Cwmaman as the first light of day was beginning to illuminate the sky. They were met at the village station by Sergeant Richards who led them to the police station which he and his family also called home. While Arthur and his knights devoured a feast fit for a king before setting off on their hunt, Nicholls and Canning breakfasted on bacon and eggs before beginning their own investigation in earnest.

When the men from New Scotland Yard had disembarked from the coal train in the fading darkness of that sharp Tuesday morning they were most likely unaware that they had arrived in a community little older than themselves. Certainly when Nicholls' father had bawled his first in the London parish of St Luke's, the village of Garnant 200 miles to the west on the banks of the River Amman in the rich green foothills of the Black Mountain and the Brecon Beacons had not yet come into existence. Garnant – its name derived from the small stream that danced its way down the southern slopes of the valley to join the winding trout-filled Amman in its floor – was a shooting star of a community, which burst into life in a blaze of burning light. The fuel which fed such light and around which the lives of thousands now revolved, glistened with a pitch-pure blackness; forged under the relentless pressure of geological millennia; as perfect as the diamonds on the crown of King George. Garnant had burst forth from the earth on the back of glittering, glistening coal.

Unbeknown to the two London detectives however – and to the residents of the coal-dust-coated valley – the village was already at its zenith. Within just a few years of the two policeman returning east to the bosom of their families and the crimes, the paperwork and the promotions they would experience, Garnant would splutter and falter as its wealth and population began to ebb. When the men from Scotland Yard stepped onto the railway platform on that cold February morning, Garnant – and the Amman Valley – was at the pinnacle of its hustling, bustling, existence, but the act which had brought them there would come to symbolise the tipping point for a village so deeply grounded in the earth. The days, weeks and years which were to follow the murder of Thomas Thomas would witness – imperceptibly at first, but relentlessly, inevitably – the beginning of the slow decline of a community and the demise of the industry which nourished it. By the time of the detectives' arrival, the River Amman ran thick and black with the evidence of a landscape's exploitation and the trout were all long gone.

Garnant exploded into life with all the combustive immediacy of the deadly gases which lurked among the workings underground. The bounty of the South Wales coalfield had powered an empire on which the sun never set. The reach of British influence had stretched from the Americas in the west to

India and the Orient, and it had done so thanks to the energy stored within the fossilised carbon layers found beneath the ground, from the Amman and Gwendraeth valleys in the west to Ebbw Vale in the east. From Jamaica to Bombay, the expansion of the empire had been fuelled by coal. The most productive, most efficient, most sought after and subsequently, most valuable of which, was anthracite, a hard, compact variety mined around the villages of Garnant, Glanaman, Betws and Llandybie. Anthracite contains the highest carbon content of any coal – between 92 and 98 per cent, the highest calorific content and the fewest impurities. It produces the least tarry residue and gives off the fewest noxious vapours. It is denser and harder than any other coal. It has the highest lustre – a lump dug straight from the seam, glistens like polished black glass. So compact are the carbon molecules in the anthracite of Cwmaman that a lump can be lifted from the earth and drawn down a freshly laundered white cotton shirt without leaving so much as a smudge. Amman Valley anthracite is valued in the top one per cent of the world's coal deposits. It is the finest coal on earth.

By the middle years of Queen Victoria's reign, anthracite hewn with pick and shovel from within Cwmaman was already known to be the most valuable power source known to man. It heated homes, powered engines, and fuelled the British dominance of the globe. The Amman Valley grew fat and rich as the unceasing demand for the black gold beneath its rolling slopes expanded exponentially throughout the late nineteenth and early twentieth centuries. Though the anthracite itself was clean and hard, the job of extracting it from the ground was filthy, back-breaking work, but the promise it offered saw men flock from near and far to harvest the rich bounty of this land. When Victoria had come to the throne in 1838, there had been no Garnant or Glanaman. There was simply Cwmaman – the Amman Valley. Between Ammanford in the west and Gwaun cae Gurwen to the east, the five-mile valley course had boasted just a scattering of homes and a population numbering in the low hundreds, composed mainly of farm workers and their families. There was no road east or west and the only access came down from the mountain road which linked the droving town of Llandeilo to the north with Brynaman in the east. That road followed the summit of the hills that marked the northern limit of the valley, and from a point above what would one day become the twin villages of Garnant and Glanaman, a track descended down to the River Amman and offered valley residents their main means of transport, communication and escape.

There was also a small population of coal-miners, who toiled and sweated at those points where geology and geography had combined to tear open the topsoil at isolated spots along the valley sides like the crust of a freshly-baked loaf and expose the rich black seams which had remained untouched beneath the ground for 300 million years. In the early days of industry, men had dug what they could from the climbing slopes with spade and pick, loaded their haul into buckets to heat their homes or onto the backs of ponies to walk their treasure along the muddy banks of the river to Ammanford – still then just a village known only by the name of its pub, Cross Inn – or east to the head of the Swansea Valley and on to the small towns which ran south down towards the sea. Mining, in one primitive form or another, had taken place in the valley since the Middle Ages and the first record of a mine appears in 1757, but for the following fifty to eighty years, the energy and effort expended in the harvest were of greater value than the resource being produced.

The population of the valley remained in the hundreds throughout the early 1800s as each generation succeeded the last. Numbers rose to slightly more than 1,000 for the first time by the middle of the century, but then the universe that was Cwmaman expanded exponentially as if the God Almighty, worshipped every Sunday at Hen Bethel Chapel, had intoned the incantation, Let There be Light. And there was light – the light of steel and steam; the light of modernity and industry. The light that sparked the birth of Garnant and Glanaman was found in the orange glow of the steam train's firebox.

The railway arrived in Cwmaman on April 10, 1840. The Llanelly Railway and Dock Company line linking Pontarddulais to Cwmaman via Ammanford opened the valley to the world for the first time, and the world was happy to take advantage and suck whatever bounty it could find from the quiet, rural landscape. The railway provided the small-scale mining operations with a direct link to the tin-works of Llanelli and the docks of Swansea and beyond. Its arrival signalled the coming boom in industry, people and wealth. Passengers and goods rolled in while coal – valuable Cwmaman anthracite – began to leave in quantities far in excess of what had gone before, and the economics of industry began to feed a ravenous hunger for the rich minerals locked beneath the valley floor. The line was extended south-east to Gwaun cae Gurwen just thirteen months later and by the summer of 1842, the station at Cwmaman – initially little more than a platform in what was to become the village of Garnant – became a key junction due to the opening of a secondary branch line north-east to Brynaman.

The growth of the valley economy required a bigger and better service, and a new, improved station was built. In a short time, the station at Garnant was expanded, and a second was built just a mile or so to the west. The Cross Keys station, named after the public house nearby, was soon renamed Glanaman. Like their neighbours at Cross Inn, the God-fearing residents of the valley had no desire for their community to be known across the nation by the name of an alehouse. At a stroke, a disparate agrarian valley community gave birth to two thriving industrial villages. The introduction of the railway presented the opportunity for the modernisation and industrialisation of the Amman Valley at a rate previously unimaginable. What were once only tiny pits providing work to just a handful of men were, within the space of a few years and as a result of advances in mining technology, transformed into major excavations producing thousands of tonnes of coal a day and requiring a workforce of hundreds. The thirst of the Empire for Amman valley anthracite would not be quenched and the more Cwmaman produced, the more the outside world demanded.

Where previously coal had been hacked from exposed seams using rudimentary tools and naked geology, shafts were sunk and full-sized collieries opened. Garnant Colliery at the eastern end of the valley had been in operation to some degree since the middle of the 1830s, but the enhanced transportation links allowed it to become more productive – and more profitable – and with every extra pound earned the colliery expanded. By the mid 1840s, other mines were being sunk, and, in 1854, Raven Colliery – taking its named from the family emblem of the

Dynevor family, which owned the land of Cwmaman – was opened. Raven was a massive undertaking which would, at its peak, employ almost 500 men – more than every man, woman and child living in the valley just 50 years earlier. Mining – even with modern techniques – remained a dangerous, back-breaking toil, but men continued to swell the valley population with the promise of work and wages. The first dedicated passenger service through Cwmaman was opened on May 1, 1850, and by 1869 the Llanelly Railway and Dock Company was running a twice-daily service into Garnant. The company was taken over by The Great Western Railway on January 1, 1873, but the thirty years since its opening had seen the population of the valley double from 500 or 600 to 1,100. Those residents who found themselves concerned by the sudden transformation of the pastoral life of their childhoods into dust-coated fire-belching industrial heartland had however seen nothing yet.

While coal provided the foundation of both Garnant and Glanamman, feeding the economy with cash and consumers, tinplate would see both population and purchasing-power rocket. Processed iron created steel, but the metal of the future proved vulnerable to that most ancient of enemies – the elements. Exposure to the air caused it to corrode and rust, and so it required coating with something less susceptible to the gnawing moisture and atmospheric conditions. The problem of protecting steel gave birth to an industry of its own – tinplating. By the middle of the nineteenth century, Llanelli was already well on its way to becoming the tinplate capital of the world, earning it the nickname Tinopolis, and the availability of the raw materials required to produce tinplate meant that Cwmaman was equally well-suited to the industry. The Amman Tinworks was built at Garnant on the southern banks of the River Amman in 1882. The venture had come with a blessing from God, and the vicar of Christchurch laid the foundation stone in May of that year. Operations at the works began in earnest in 1883. Meanwhile, yet another giant new colliery – Gellyceidrim – was opened between Garnant and Glanaman in 1891. It would – in time – become the largest, most productive mine in the valley.

The expansion of the operations and the opening of the tinworks catapulted Cwmaman into a thriving hub of industry and each passing decade saw only further expansion – of indus-try and people. By 1901, the combined population of Garnant and Glanaman had risen to more than 2,400 as word spread that work was available in the rural west. Men flocked from London, the Midlands, the north of England, Scotland and beyond in search of a wage. By 1910, Garnant station was receiving seven passenger trains a day from Monday to Saturday, and two on Sundays. The population had again doubled with the number of adult residents now numbering 4,777. In 1903, the station had issued 32,735 passenger tickets. In 1913, the figure had risen to 76,491 – almost 1,500 each week as the valley residents took advantage of the money in their pockets and the opportunities to spread their wings on day trips to Carmarthen, Swansea, Llanelli and beyond. Meanwhile, the train's role of delivering mail to the swelling numbers of incomers rocketed from 4,257 parcels handled in 1903 to more than 9,000 a decade later. Garnant, Glanaman and the entire Amman Valley were riding the crest of wave. And while the railway provided the oxygen in which Garnant thrived, it was coal that continued to be the fuel the economy. In 1903, 102,696 tonnes of coal passed through Garnant station. Ten years later, the figure has risen to more than 200,000. When Nicholls and Canning stepped onto Garnant station platform on February 15, 1921, the population of Cwmaman was at an all-time high of 5,302.

The five-mile valley – from Ammanford to Gwaun cae Gurwen – was home to almost 21,000 souls, and at its heart, the twin villages of Garnant and Glanaman were heaving, throbbing centres of industry and commerce which men like Morgan Jeffreys were able to exploit. With thousands of working men with a good wage in their pockets, a host of opportunities sprang out of the soil to help relieve them of the weight of that burden. By 1920, there were at least 70 separate businesses registered in Garnant. Glanaman offered another 54. From confectioners to cabinet-makers, shoe shops to sheet-music sellers, Garnant and Glanaman were alive with trade, services and the exchange of money. Garnant was host to six greengrocers and four fruiter-ers; there were seven drapers, three tailors and four boot-makers. The village was home to a hairdresser, six general stores, four ironmongers, a chemist and a dedicated china-ware shop. There were two butchers, a miller, a saddler and a black-smith. There was also a Post Office, two stationary outlets and two newsagents. The village had its own architects, lawyers and a doctor. Garnant had branches of four of the major British banks, a Co-operative store and at least six registered public houses, though ale was also available unofficially from dozens of residential homes who made and sold their own brew. Within a 15-minute walk, Glanaman boasted an equally diverse and vibrant economy. But this bubble was set to burst.

When the two Scotland Yard policemen arrived in West Wales, they stepped off the train into a bustling community as active and vibrant as any of the London boroughs they had left behind. Men and women from across the nation worked, earned, lived, loved and fought in numbers beyond the imaginings of those who had been born in Cwmaman just a generation or two previously. The Amman Valley would never see such life – or such wealth – again. As surely as the life had ebbed from Thomas Thomas on the floor of Star Stores, so too had the twin villages began to lose their fight for breath. As the frail, deaf shopkeeper lay bleeding, so the shooting star that was the Amman Valley reached its zenith and began to fall. Decline set in quickly as the world came to terms with life after the Great War. Within two years of the detectives' return to Scotland Yard, rail passenger tickets would fall to 45,036 in 1923, the number of parcels dealt with at the station dropped from 9,033 to 6,553 and, most tellingly of all, the quantity of coal handled – the fuel which fired and fed the entire community – would plummet by more than half to 91,952 – less even than the days before the century had turned.

Chapter Six:
A day like any other

INSPECTOR NICHOLLS AND Detective Sergeant Canning welcomed the bacon and eggs that awaited them as warmly as they were greeted by the residents of Garnant Police Station. While housing the village station on the ground floor with an office, a reception area and a cell, the building was also the home of Sergeant Richards, his wife Mary, PC Thomas, his wife Annie and their respective families. It therefore came as little surprise to the men from Scotland Yard when they found themselves the centre of attention for prying young eyes of the youngest children of the station who peered around the door jambs before being shooed away by their mothers who scurried from kitchen to dining room with second helpings and cups of hot, sweet tea. With their breakfast plates cleared and despite the fatigue of their overnight journey, the two detectives were keen to be brought up to speed on the details of the case and all developments since Nicholls had spoken with the Chief Constable by telephone the previous afternoon.

Thomas Richards had been far from idle as he had nervously awaited the arrival of the men from the Criminal Investigation Department. After carrying out the search of the field to the rear of the Star Stores, he set about – as best he was able – cataloguing the day's events leading up to the murder of the shopkeeper. His task had been made somewhat easier by the fact that two of his children – 17-year-old Nellie and 14-year-old Emlyn – made up almost half of the Star's five surviving members of staff. From the information he could ascertain, the day had proceeded without incident save for a minor accident which left a window pane broken and the appearance of a number of customers late in the afternoon who appeared to have been slightly intoxicated. Mr Thomas had opened the shop at 9am as usual and the morning's trade had progressed without any event of note. Also present from opening time onwards was the first hand Phoebe Jones, Nellie and the two boy assistants Henry Morris, aged 15, and Emlyn. The errand boy Trevor Morgan spent the day in and out of the shop, delivering orders on his bicycle before returning to collect his next load. Trade had been brisk, though the shop had been no more or no less busy than was usual on a Saturday morning, with many of the regular customers coming in to buy provisions, place orders or pay outstanding bills for goods already delivered. No-one out of the ordinary had appeared and no member of the staff could recall serving anyone they considered out of the ordinary or in any way unusual. Sometime between 10am and 11am Mr Thomas had knocked over a window display of tin cans while reaching for some item, the falling cans had broken the street window behind the provisions counter. Trevor Morgan, who was waiting for Nellie Richards to put together his next delivery, was sent down to the cellar for a suitable piece of wood to cover the broken pane until a better resolution could be found. Mr Thomas himself had fastened the board over the cracked window and cleared up the broken glass. At 1pm the shop was closed for a lunch break, re-opening again as usual at 2pm.

Late in the afternoon, Nellie had left the store to make a number of deliveries of her own, returning at around 5.45pm. During her absence, various individuals entered the shop in a slightly inebriated state. Mr Thomas, as a religious man, did not approve of those who consumed intoxicating liquor, but had been willing enough to serve the customers and take their money as none appeared to be in a state of actual drunkenness despite smelling of alcohol. The individuals in question were all local men and regular customers at the Star who had attended the rugby match played earlier at Cwmaman Park. At about 6pm the various members of staff – apart from Mr Thomas – took their turn to leave the shop and go home for a short tea-break. The boys and Nellie had all used the side entrance when leaving. Phoebe Jones had gone out through the cellar door to make the short trip to her lodgings with the Jeffreys family at nearby Commerce House. Sometime after Phoebe had returned, though she could not offer a specific time, Thomas Conway Morgan, an occasional customer at Star Stores, had entered through the main street door and spoken with Mr Thomas about the possibility of taking a wooden box. Mr Thomas often allowed customers to reserve boxes to fill with their purchases and it was not in any way unusual for him to allow such customers to the cellar, sometimes accompanied and sometimes alone, to select a box of their choice. These customers would usually then leave the shop by the cellar door.

Phoebe had a clear recollection of Mr Morgan, a man with whom Sergeant Richards was all too familiar, going to the cellar in search of such a box as she was not altogether comfortable in his presence due to his reputation in the village as a thief. A deformity to his right hand only added to her unease in his company. On Saturday night, at least half a dozen regular customers had gone down into the cellar to choose a box and then left either by the cellar door or returned up the stairs to leave by the main entrance. Shortly after 7.30pm, Morgan Jeffreys senior had entered the shop and purchased various items. He was on the premises for ten to fifteen minutes before leaving, but none of the shop staff could recall whether he had left by the main door or had gone out through the cellar. Between 7.45pm and 8pm, Mr Thomas Mountstephens and his wife Lily had come in with their two sons and remained for approximately ten minutes during which time they settled a bill for goods which had been delivered earlier in the day by the errand boy. The couple, though they did not speak with any member of staff save for the shop manager himself, were well known to the various assistants as Mr Thomas, and the previous manager before him, lodged with the couple at Glanyrafon Villas.

At 8.15pm Thomas Thomas closed the shop, locked the door and doused the two window lights. The shop's remaining 14 gas lights would not be extinguished until he left for the night. Henry Morris then fixed the portable gate in the porch outside the front door and re-entered the shop from the side staff door between the Star and Mrs Smith's fruit shop. For the next thirty minutes or so, the shop staff had gone about their end of day chores with the boys taking the bucket full of floor sweepings to the cellar and emptying them into the wooden box near the rear door. Emlyn Richards had then leant the shop broom, with the head uppermost, against the wall next to the safe.

At approximately 8.45pm, Nellie had run her errand and returned by the cellar door, securing it behind her. She, along with the three boys, then left by the side door while Phoebe made up the shop ledgers and reckoned the day's takings from the receipts with Mr Thomas. The job took her a little over an hour to check and then double-check, as was demanded by Mr Thomas.

The shopkeeper took off his apron and shop coat, placing them on a hook near the warehouse door, before he emptied the tills of money and settled behind the grocery counter with the shop cash book and the weekly accounts. Phoebe left by the side door at 9.45pm and went up the little corridor, through the outer door and on to the valley road. Before she departed, Mr Thomas, as was his habit, asked her to check the cellar door was locked. Phoebe went to the top of the cellar stairs and, from where stood – despite there being no light in the cellar – she could, thanks to the illumination of the shop lights behind her –see that the door had been both locked and then bolted with an iron bar used specifically for the purpose. She then left by the side door, slamming it hard behind her to ensure the bolt caught in the latch thereby ensuring it could only be opened from inside. Mr Thomas was still standing at the grocery counter with the cash book, the day's takings and the two small tins into which he would eventually place the cash, laid out in front of him.

Sergeant Richards was satisfied that he had been able to brief the men from Scotland Yard fully on the events leading up to the murder at the Star and the visitors from London appeared impressed by his conscientious efforts. The four officers, two in uniform and two in London suits, sat around the kitchen table sipping tea from the finest china cups the ladies of the station had available as PS Richards and PC Thomas gave what information they could and answered whatever questions the men from Scotland Yard put to them. They returned at various points to specific aspects of the sergeant's notes, clarifying and assessing points of interest. Both Garnant officers were pleased with their efforts. Nicholls was impressed too. He had come to Garnant doubtful of the efficiency of these local Welsh Bobbies and fearful that their inadequacies might well impede the investigation rather that progress it. Instead, he had found two men who – despite the limitations of their equipment and training– appeared dedicated and professional. Sergeant Richards in particular left Nicholls confident that no obvious clue had been missed nor ruined by clumsy fingers or naive over-enthusiasm. He was however dismayed to learn that the scene of the crime had been scrubbed clean by the good ladies of Garnant. Richards also felt it right to inform the detectives that, though no obvious clues or evidence had linked either man to the crime, both Morgan Jeffreys, the landlord of Star Stores and owner of Commerce Place, and Thomas Mountstephens, the dead man's landlord, were the subject of local rumour and already various fingers were pointing in the direction of both men. There was also speculation as to whether a local man, known to have a history as a petty thief and who had been seen in the Star that day, was somehow involved. Nicholls nodded sagely, but said he would rather wait to see where the evidence might lead rather than follow on the trail of gossip and speculation.

Richards produced the boning knife and broom handle retrieved from the brook for inspection. Two nails protruded from the end of the broom handle and it seemed safe and logical to assume that these had previously secured the broomhead to the stick. A visual comparison confirmed Richards' assessment that the protruding nails fitting neatly into the void in the broomhead created by the splintering of the wood during a heavy impact. Satisfied that the evidence – as it was – had been kept secure and untouched in the station strongbox, Nicholls asked what other leads might have come to the fore. The only fresh line enquiry to have emerged since his conversation with the Chief Constable had arrived late on Monday afternoon when a gentleman from Ammanford had presented himself at the station. He was interviewed by Sergeant Richards who learned that the man had attended the same concert as Phoebe Jones on Saturday night. The gentleman had then set out on his homeward journey in his motorcar but had stopped a short distance east of the Star Stores to pick up a lone hitchhiker who was walking along the valley road in the direction of Ammanford. The time had been approximately 2am. The motorist had happily given the man a lift for the night had been cold with a freezing mist settling along the valley basin. Driver and passenger had chatted amiably enough during the short journey before the hitchhiker was dropped – as requested – at Tirydail Square in Ammanford a short time later. The driver had no recollection of ever seeing his passenger before though he claimed to have attended the same concert at Stepney Hall. Nor did he recognise him as a resident of Ammanford though he had aroused no suspicion walking home so late as the last bus had long since made its final journey for the evening. The driver had shown no great concern or seen any reason to doubt his passenger as at that stage he was unaware of the events which had occurred earlier in the evening at the Star. The two men had shared little more than idle chatter and had not exchanged names or any other information which might further identify the pedestrian, their conversation centring solely on the weather, the driving conditions and the joys of owning a car. The fact that this man had remained in Garnant for some three hours after the dance had ended at 11pm was a cause of some suspicion for Sergeant Richards. Nicholls agreed it was imperative that the hitchhiker be traced with all haste.

Nicholls was keen to visit the scene of the murder at the earliest opportunity in the hope that the cleaners might have left some vital clue untouched and after finishing breakfast the four men walked the short distance to Star Stores. The arrival of the detectives had not gone unnoticed amongst the village gossips and had already caused a flurry of interest among residents. As the four men made their way along the valley road, the people of Garnant and Glanaman whispered and pointed as they passed, a crowd of onlookers following in their footsteps with its numbers swelling at each step. The Deputy Chief Constable had arranged to travel over from Llandeilo at 10am to discuss the case ahead of the opening of the inquest and the Scotland Yard detectives wished to fully familiarise themselves with the shop and surrounding area before the meeting. As he led the men from London along the valley road, Richards tried as best as he was able to give them a better understanding of the layout and geography of the village, pointing out key locations, such as the collieries, pubs and key businesses, explaining road layouts and access points.

Sergeant Richards was extremely keen to show Nicholls

what, he considered, might be the only clue to have been found inside the Star. Nicholls however was aware of the need for patience. He had seen previously how excited local officers, unfamiliar with the necessity of patient, methodical investigation required in a murder inquiry, had gone rushing past the seemingly insignificant which might later prove crucial. Those unused to murder often operated with every expectation of having the case unravel before their eyes. Nicholls knew better than most that homicide investigations were rarely so simple. He knew that it was essential he keep a completely open mind in relation to all aspects of the inquiry. What at first might be considered a clue could later prove unconnected or irrelevant to the investigation at hand, what might initially be thought so insignificant as to be ignored by the first officers on the scene would often become the key to unlocking the whole mystery. Despite the keenness of Sergeant Richards to get him inside the store and away from the prying eyes of the following crowd, Nicholls asked that he first be shown the broken, boarded window pane which Thomas Thomas had fixed in the hours prior to his death.

With the detectives noting down the details in their pocket books, Richards then guided them down Coronation Arcade to the yard at the rear of the Star where, in response to the questions of his new companions, he highlighted the complete absence of any footprints which might have been linked to the crime and the perpetrator's subsequent departure from the scene. Nicholls was again satisfied that the uniformed officer's assessment was correct that there had been little or no chance of any boot impressions being left due to the heavily compacted earth and sub-zero temperature overnight. With the examination of the area to the rear of the shop complete, Richards ushered them to the cellar door through which the killer had most likely escaped, and from there up into the heart of the Star.

Once inside the shop, the detectives carried out a minute examination of the floor, scouring every inch in search of marks or bloodstains which might have been missed by the good ladies of Garnant but could offer some insight into the onslaught which had occurred there. Despite their best effort with naked eye and magnifying glass, they found nothing beyond that which the sergeant had already noted. The wooden box on which the shopkeeper's vital fluid had been splashed, was still stained with blood despite the obvious attentions of a scrubbing brush and considerable effort. The stains had lost all definition due to the toil of the unwelcome cleaners, but what remained provided a clear indication of the brutality of the attack. With little else to see, the detectives expanded their search to the remainder of the shop, warehouse and cellar area. During their examination, Nicholls inspected the smudges and grease marks on various surfaces including the shelving fixed to the wall behind the provisions counter and on the counter itself highlighted by Richards. After viewing under his eye glass, he agreed with the Garnant man's identification of a number of fingerprints. Canning was then given the task of coating the prints in a fine black powder and securing the area in which they were located ahead of their being photographed.

Nicholls and the two Carmarthenshire officers then examined each of the doors and windows of the Star and – apart from the broken window pane – could find nothing untoward. There appeared no sign of forced entry anywhere on the premises. It was agreed that the only means of escape had been through the open rear door. Only after he was satisfied that nothing had been missed during previous searches did Nicholls allow Richards to direct his attention to the safe and the one item which the sergeant believed may have been worthy of consideration as a clue.

During his initial examination of the open safe in the hours following the discovery of the body, Richards had spotted a small piece of a broken button lodged in the lower of the two mortises inside the right-hand side of the safe. The broken button appeared to be one such as might have been found on a waistcoat, a coat sleeve or possibly the cuff of a shirt. Richards surmised that the thief may possibly have caught his sleeve or some other item of clothing on the safe lock as he had reached in to remove the money tins, causing the button to snap. It was possible, Richards suggested, that the broken button had then fallen unnoticed by the killer and lodged in the mortise of the safe door. Although Nicholls agreed that the idea was solid, by testing the door it became clear that the officers were able to open and close the safe while the broken button remained lodged in its place without causing any hindrance to the movement or mechanism. It was therefore decided that while it was certainly possible that the button had broken from the killer's clothing, it was just as likely to have been present and gone unnoticed long before the crime had been committed. It would however be sensible to examine any suspect's clothes in the hope of finding what remained of the button still attached to a garment.

Taking out his magnifying glass again, Nicholls then began a minute inspection of the safe both inside and out, again finding numerous fingerprints and greasy smears – particularly on and around the door and lock. His expert eye however left him of the opinion that the marks were "poorly defined and unlikely to prove useful" having been subjected to fingers being repeatedly placed at the same point, overlaying print on top of print and making them impossible to separate into distinct marks. From what was known of the habits of the shopkeeper, and the fact that the ledger books remained open on the grocery counter, it seemed extremely likely that the thief had found the safe door open and would therefore have had no need to touch any part of the steel box itself. He would simply have had to reach in through the open door and take whatever he chose from inside. The two tins in which the shop takings were kept, and which were found lying at the side and in front of the safe were also carefully examined under Nicholls' magnifying glass. The larger tin, in which the shopkeeper had kept the silver, appeared to have fingerprints on the inside at each end. However the marks on one end were again overlayed and superimposed with print on top of print due to repeated handling. Again, the inspector concluded, the marks would prove too indistinct and smudged, making it impossible to isolate one from another. Those at the other end were slightly clearer and less smudged through multiple handlings though were also, in Nicholls' expert opinion, lacking definition and "of poor character". In spite of his reservations, he withdrew a small container of black powder from his pocket and, while the Carmarthenshire men watched closely, sprinkled some of the contents over what he considered to be the more distinct of the finger impressions. While the powder made him able to improve the contrast of the prints against the metal of the container, Nicholls again formed the opinion that the marks would be of little use – unless they were able to identify a suspect whose own fingerprints could be taken and tested in comparison. Nonetheless – and with little else to take from the scene, he ordered Sergeant Richards to carefully remove the tin and store it under lock and key at the station ahead of such an eventuality or the possibility that in the coming days he might change his mind and have the container despatched to London for more scientific analysis. With their examination complete, the four men returned to the station to await the arrival of the Deputy Chief Constable. While it had been useful for the men from Scotland Yard to have first-hand experience of the scene and absorb the layout of the shop – its entrances and exits and the positioning of the counters, the stairs to the cellar and the like – little else had been gained from the tour of Star Stores.

The meeting with Deputy Chief Constable Evans did not got as well as Nicholls had hoped. Despite the discovery of the murder weapons, the broken button and possible – albeit imperfect – fingerprints, Evans was already expressing doubt that the crime would ever be solved. "As far as I can see, there remains not a single worthwhile clue for the police to work upon," he told the man from Scotland Yard.

Evans was 65 years old and less than two months from retirement. It seemed to Nicholls that perhaps the Deputy Chief Inspector was already thinking of his garden and his pipe, though he chose not to share such thoughts with the local officers. It did though seem to Nicholls that Evans had given up the chase before the hunt had even begun. The Deputy Chief Constable did however place at Nicholls' disposal "the full assistance" of the Carmarthenshire Constabulary to investigate the crime in whatever manner he saw fit. Evans was aware that although he felt there was little chance of an arrest it would be unacceptable in the eyes of the people of the county to say so publicly, or provide so little support to the men from Scotland Yard as to make it clear that he felt they had come to South Wales on little more than a fool's errand. Nicholls wondered whether Evans was more keen to see himself and Canning return to London on the earliest train possible to reduce any bill the Carmarthenshire Constabulary might face for their services than he was concerned about apprehending a killer. In reality, the full assistance of the Carmarthenshire Constabulary amounted to Sergeant Richards and Constable Thomas being made available for the remainder of his time in the valley. Nicholls was assured that should there be some form of break-through in the case "any other assistance that he might require would be readily given", but for the day-to-day ground-work of the investigation he should look no further than the support provided by the two Garnant officers. With little more to be gained from further discussions, Nicholls, Canning, Sergeant Richards, PC Thomas and Deputy Chief Constable Evans made their way to New Bethel Chapel where John William Nicholas, the Carmarthen County Council solicitor and clerk to the county finance committee, was – in his role as county Coroner – about to open the inquest into the death of Thomas Thomas.

Chapter Seven:
A case beyond control

THE SPACIOUS VESTRY at the rear of New Bethel Chapel was already crowded when Nicholls, Canning, Sergeant Richards, PC Thomas and Deputy Chief Constable Evans arrived at its gates. As many residents of Garnant as were able had already pushed their way inside to hear what might be said. A sea of those who had arrived too late pressed forward in the entrance way but separated like the waters before Moses as the men from Scotland Yard approached. Those who had not been at the earlier visit to the scene of the crime strained and shoved, keen to catch a first glimpse of the detectives. The chapel itself was just two hundred or so yards down the valley road in the direction of Ammanford from the Star and sat on the boundery between Garnant and Glanaman. It had been built with the purpose of serving the Non-Conformist faithful of both villages and had been erected on land gifted for the purpose by Evan Daniel of Swansea. The chapel, built at a reported cost of £2,040 11s and 6d, had been opened in 1876 following the laying of the foundation stone two years earlier and became one of the most well attended chapels in Wales, with services regularly boasting a congregation numbering in excess of 1,300 worshippers. In 1914 a new organ was constructed for the princely fee of £1,000 – mainly due to the efforts of the Organ Fund Committee's energetic secretary, William Michael – the husband of Margaret Michael, whom Diana Bowen had breathlessly told her tale of awful screams and boys with hands caught in bacon slicers while Thomas Thomas lay dying.

A hush fell on the crowded vestry and all eyes turned towards Inspector Nicholls and his colleagues as they entered and took their seats beside the gathered pressman. John Nicholas then appeared to take his place at a table under the pulpit and call the proceedings to order. Once the formalities of swearing in the eight man jury – with John Phillips, postmaster of Glanaman, as its foreman – were over, the Coroner eyed them each in turn.

"You are sworn to inquire into the circumstances attending the death of Thomas Thomas," he told them solemnly. "All I think is necessary today is to simply take evidence of identification," he added. The reverential hush amongst the sardine-tight crowd turned to a groan as those gathered realised there would be no great revelations this morning. With a scolding glance around the room, the Coroner offered only the explanation that the day's proceedings would be unable to throw new light on the crime due to the strictest secrecy of the ongoing police investigation. He explained his expectations for the hearing to ensure none would be in any doubt as to the legal processes ahead.

"I shall then adjourn the enquiry until some convenient day, in order that the police, after making further investigation – we hope with some result – may be able to place before the Court a continuous, consecutive and strong story," he said. "I think it better to do that than call part of the evidence now and part again."

However, before any evidence was taken or the one witness of the day called, the Coroner and jurors were taken to Glanyrafon Villas where the body of Thomas Thomas remained so that they might view the corpse and see for themselves the gruesome injuries he had suffered. Upon their return to New Bethel Chapel and the calling once again to order, the sole witness was sworn in. He gave his name as John Thomas, only brother of deceased. He told the court that he lived at Blackpill in Swansea, and was employed by the London and North West Railway company as stationmaster at Mumbles Road. John Thomas confirmed that the dead man was indeed his brother Thomas, who was two months short of his forty-fifth birthday at the time of his death. His brother was, John Thomas said, a bachelor who has been employed by the Star Tea Company as a store manager for some fourteen years, first at Bridgend, then Llandeilo and latterly at Garnant.

"What was his condition as to health?" asked the Coroner.

"Fair," replied the witness, "though he was never very robust."

He then went on to describe the numerous ailments suffered by his brother throughout his life: the headaches and varicose veins; the deafness in one ear and partial deafness of the other;

the nasal difficulties which had required surgery just a week prior to the murder. John Thomas said he had last seen his brother alive when the latter had visited him and his wife in Swansea some six or so weeks earlier, with the shopkeeper having spent the Christmas holiday at their home. With confirmation of Thomas Thomas' identity complete, John Nicholas – Coroner to the County of Carmarthenshire – adjourned the inquest until a second hearing on March 1, when he hoped the full facts of the case would be cast into the light of the public's gaze and the identity of the killer at last revealed.

With the formalities complete and the Coroner departed, the gathered pressman crowded and jostled around the detetcives from Scotland Yard in some hope of a quote. The nature of the questions coming from the *Amman Valley Chronicle*'s reporter caused Nicholls a growing sense of unease. It became all too clear to him that Dr Jones had already been interviewed and given an indication of his preliminary findings. Nicholls heart sank even lower when he learned that Thomas Mountstephens, the dead man's landlord, had also already received a visit from the press. Canning dispatched everyone else from the vestry save for the man from the *Chronicle* before Nicholls demanded to know exactly what the doctor had said, and more importantly, what the newspaper planned to print. The reporter admitted he had spoken with the doctor on the Sunday evening after his initial viewing of the body but prior to the full post-mortem examination.

"Dr. Jones said he was called to the shop about ten o'clock on Sunday morning and saw the deceased lying behind the counter with his head towards the window," the reporter told them.

Flicking through his notepad, he read the quotes he had taken down during the conversation. "On a superficial examination I found a gap in the throat, which had severed the carotid artery and the jugular vein. There was also a puncture wound in the abdomen."

The newsman reeled off a list of the dead man's injuries as Nicholls and Canning glanced at each other in horror. They would have much preferred to keep such findings to themselves for the time being.

"The puncture wounds were done with a sharp instrument,

and the bruises may have been caused by the brush. Either of these wounds would ultimately prove fatal, but the immediate fatal wound was the gash in the throat, from which he would bleed quickly to death," the reporter continued. "The wound in the throat was about one inch by one inch and death would come in the course of a few seconds."

Nicholls shook his head and wondered what other evidence and details of the case which could in time have proved essential to the investigation had already been made public. His worst fears were soon to be confirmed. Turning his page, the reporter continued.

"The peculiar part of the wound in the abdomen was that none of the clothing was cut," he read. "The top buttons of the trousers were opened and also part of the waistcoat. The shirt had been uplifted, and there was a punctured wound with a couple of scratches round about it."

Crucial information about the nature of the crime which should have been known only to the police and the killer would be common knowledge within days, if it was not already. To make matters worse, the reporter flicked another page and continued.

"It would have been an easy matter for the murderer to have followed the deceased upstairs and then felled him," the doctor had said. "The first blow apparently only stunned the deceased, leading to the conclusion that Thomas Thomas must then have recognised his assailant. On his partial recovery another scuffle seems to have taken place, with the result that the murderer got hold of the broom handle lying at the time on the floor and belaboured the deceased with it. The knife was eventually brought into use."

With the details of their case already public knowledge before they had even arrived on the scene and set to be published in the valley newspaper, the two Scotland Yard detectives began to wonder whether the investigation was already beyond their control.

Nicholls was furious. Specific details of the crime had not just been leaked to the press, but thanks to Dr Jones, had gushed out in a torrent. Minute aspects of the case which should by right have only been known to the police and the killer would be available for every Tom, Dick and Harry to read when the *Amman Valley Chronicle* went on sale in less than 48 hours time. Nicholls' experience told him that it was often an intimate knowledge of a crime which could catch a killer. With the right encouragement, a suspect might be encouraged to entrap himself with details to which only someone at the scene would have been privy. Thanks to the good doctor, those details would now be the central topic of conversation and gossip up and down the valley. Crucial information such as the unbuttoning of the clothing would, it seemed to the detective, have been a trump card in the questioning of a suspect as they closed in on the culprit. Their ace however was now lying face up on the table for all to see. He was further disturbed that the doctor had decided to inform the press of his assessment of the order of events based on the injuries before detailing his theory to the police. Both Nicholls and Canning were aware that the calculating of the correct timing of the injuries and the order in which they were inflicted often proved crucial in attaining a conviction for murder and yet Dr Jones had broadcast his professional medical opinion to the world at large. The mood of the man from Scotland Yard was further darkened when he realised that the only photographs of the scene had been taken by the *Chronicle*'s photographer and they too would be appearing in Thursday's edition of the newspaper. In a bid to reclaim some slim aspect of control over the investigation – however minor, Nicholls asked Sergeant Richards who he considered the best photographer in the region. PC Thomas was then despatched to Ammanford to secure the services of Mr William Matthews, Photographer, of The Arcade, Ammanford. Matthews returned with Thomas and took pictures of the interior and exterior of the crime scene along with images of the dusted fingerprints identified by Canning's powder before joining Nicholls and his colleague at Two Glanyrafon Villas where he set about photographing the mutilated body of Thomas Thomas.

Even by the standards of Scotland Yard's elite Criminal Investigation Department, George Robert Nicholls was not your average policeman. By the time he had left school, Nicholls was fluent in both French and German, and at the age of fourteen was employed as a barrister's clerk with the New Securities

Corporation at Finsbury House, Blomfield Street, on the edge of the City of London's Square Mile – the financial centre of the Empire. The position was merely a temporary means to an end for Nicholls however and a career in high finance held no interest for him. On the turning of his twenty-first birthday – the minimum age acceptable for applications to the Metropolitan Police – the Islington boy followed in the footsteps of his maternal grandfather William Haines and applied to join the Force.

After a long, frustrating recruitment process, Nicholls finally fulfilled his life-long ambition and on November 28, 1898, he became a constable of the Metropolitan Police. He was aged 21 years and 255 days and received Warrant Card number 84634. His sharp intellect and linguistic abilities were quickly noticed by his senior officers and his days amongst the uniformed ranks of the beat constables of D Division – based at Marylebone – would be short-lived. On April 24, 1900, Nicholls was transferred to the legendary plain-clothes Criminal Investigation Department, based at the Commissioner's Office in New Scotland Yard. After less than eighteen months in uniform, Nicholls became a detective in the most famous department of the most respected police force in the world.

But even amongst the ranks of the finest officers the country could boast, his meteoric rise continued. The warehouse night-watchman's son made Detective Sergeant in December 1903 and was promoted through the Force grades from third to second to Sergeant First Class by 1909. From the moment he had joined CID, his language skills were put to good use. Nicholls became the Met's expert on the foreign criminals and crime gangs that had flocked across the Channel in the late Victorian era and set up tight enclaves by the turn of the century, particularly those who made for London where he was a familiar face at the various haunts populated by the numerous overseas communities. His abilities also ensured he became one of the first truly international policemen and he was well known to the Police Chiefs of Paris, Berlin and beyond as crime became a cross-border problem.

It was the then Detective Sergeant Nicholls that accompanied Detective Inspector Roux of the French Police to oversee the arrest and extradition of the gambler and fraudster Charles

Wells, the man who broke the bank at Monte Carlo. Wells defrauded thousands of French citizens of millions of francs with an elaborate pyramid investment scam, but was best known for 'breaking the bank' at the casinos of Monte Carlo where, in spite of the attention of numerous private investigators employed by the casinos, was able – time and again – to beat the roulette table and empty the safe. On one audacious evening, he bet his stake on the number five. He followed up on the very next spin with exactly the same bet. Then did it again; and again. Wells bet number five five times in succession – overcoming odds of trillions to one. The trick ensured him world-wide fame as The Man Who Broke the Bank of Monte Carlo, courtesy of Fred Gilbert's music hall hit. Wells was eventually traced to the luxury yacht *Excelsior* off the coast of Falmouth in January 1912. Nicholls and Roux swooped, and Wells and his French lover – a woman half his age – were transported to London before crossing the Channel to face justice in a Parisian courtroom on fraud charges. He would ultimately die alone and penniless in Paris in 1922 following his release – his young lover having long since moved on. The secret of his success at the roulette table went with him to the grave.

Nicholls' role in the successful capture of Wells made him a celebrity and he was as much the darling of the Commissioner's Office as he was newspaper headline writers. Within a month of Wells' arrest, Nicholls was promoted to the rank of Detective Inspector (Second Class). A year later he was upgraded to First Class.

With the outbreak of the Great War, the ex-pat communities in the capital began to simmer with discontent forcing the Metropolitan Police to broaden its horizons and direct its attention beyond the normal limitations of domestic criminality. Nicholls, with his mastery of German and French and his intimate knowledge of the overseas enclaves of London, was tailor-made for the times. He was seconded to Scotland Yard's Special Branch, the specialist intelligence unit developed to counter threats of terrorism, subversion and overseas propaganda on the UK mainland. He joined the unit with an espionage and counter-espionage remit, and from 1914 until the German surrender in 1918, the nightwatchman's son took on the role as one of the nation's chief spy-catchers. As the war came to a close, his role ensuring the security of the UK mainland was rewarded with another step up the promotional ladder and he was appointed to the rank of Divisional Inspector. Nicholls experience and intelligence ensured his name remained a regular feature in the newspapers as he became the face of Scotland Yard during high-profile case after high-profile case. His regular appearances at the Old Bailey as the key prosecution witness only served to further his renown.

Prior to the murder of Thomas Thomas in Garnant, Nicholls had appeared on the front pages of newspapers from Cornwall to Dundee during the prosecution of the infamous Bamberger case, where Thelma Dorothy Bamberger, the wife of a well-known London stockbroker was eventually jailed for perjury. The scandal was the talk of post-War Britain, as Bamberger – born Lily Amelia Taylor, the daughter of an evangelist preacher – was proved a multiple adulteress, a liar, a Madam, a fraudster and a thief. She had lived an incredible criminal life, convincing her numerous lovers that it was not she, but her non-existent twin sister who had committed the litany of offences she left in her wake.

Nicholls was also Scotland Yard's chief hunter of fakes and fraudsters, and he boasted a long list of successful prosecutions of fortune-tellers, astrologists and palmistrists. But it was when investigating murder that Nicholls felt most useful to the common good.

Nicholls and Canning were already at Glanyrafon Villas when Mr Matthews, the photographer, arrived to capture the final images of Thomas Thomas' dead body. The corpse had remained in the property the deceased had shared with his landlord Thomas Mountstephens and his family, along with the lodger, Arthur Impey, after being transported there on Deputy Chief Constable Evans' instructions following its discovery on Sunday morning. It was in the Mountstephens' home that Dr George Evan Jones, assisted by Dr Trefor Rhys of Glanaman, had the previous day completed the grisly task of carrying out a post-mortem to ascertain the full extent of the dead man's injuries. The examination had taken more than three hours.

When Matthews, led by the two police officers from London,

made his way into the bedroom where the shopkeeper had slept in life and now lay in death he was met by the grim outline of a corpse draped beneath a paper shroud. From head to foot, the body had been covered in the pages of the Saturday, February 12, edition of the *Herald of Wales*, a flimsy weekly newspaper given away without charge in the Swansea area. His deathly covering was nothing more spiritual than the news on the day of his murder, though his own slaughter had come too late to be recorded. While Matthews set up his equipment, Nicholls lifted off the sheet which had covered the head of the dead man and then removed a second which blanketed the chest and stomach. The photographer, who had previously only ever taken the portraits of the living or captured the images of daily life around the Amman and Towy Valleys, fought the urge to vomit. The dead man, so frail and thin, was marble white. A piece of rolled up cardboard and one of his old white work shirts had been fashioned into a makeshift headrest. Beneath his thick brown moustache, Thomas Thomas' mouth hung open as if caught forever in the early stages of a morning yawn. His eyes stared vacantly at the ceiling. A thick band of flesh ran like a knotted cord from a rope-maker's workshop from his groin all the way up his stomach and chest and over his right shoulder in evidence of the two doctors' internal examination. Thick black thread had been used to close the body in ungainly pragmatic stitches without art or consideration and now held the remains of the dead man together. A second band of sewn flesh ran from the centre of the shopkeeper's throat up to and around the rear of his right ear. A third weaved its way from above the top of his left ear along the hairline of his scalp. The right ear and surrounding area was swollen, bruised and showed numerous small cuts and gouges. Further up the right-side of the head, close to the hairline and beneath the dead man's thin mousey brown hair the skull was misshaped and deformed and again showed a number of cuts and bruises. The discolouration of the injuries stood out all the more against the pale, cold flesh. Matthews was astounded by the thinness of the man who lay before him, the stomach was sucked in under the ribcage; the arms lacked any display of meat or muscle. Thomas Thomas was little more than skin and bone.

It was as clear to the photographer as it was to the expert eye of the policemen in his company just how easily this specimen could have been overpowered and bullied by anyone of even average strength or menace. Even the two policemen, well versed in the spectacle of death and with more than 40 years experience between them, blanched at the brutality of what lay before them. It was clear that the wounds were not limited to those which might debilitate or intimidate Thomas Thomas. The perpetrator would have been in no doubt of the result of his actions.

Once the three men gathered in the room had regained their clarity of thought, Nicholls, with the workmanlike authority he had mastered in his twenty-one years a detective, began to direct the photographer. As instructed, Matthews carefully photographed the left side of the dead man's body. He then moved his equipment to the other side of the room and set up once again, this time forever capturing the image of the right side of Thomas Thomas' broken shell and the wounds which had brought him to his end. With the photographer's work complete, the two Scotland Yard men carried out their own minute inspection of the injuries. Nicholls, at times, pulled his magnifying glass from his pocket and leaned in closely over the body, speaking of numerous points of interest to Canning who duly noted each in the small black notebook which he kept poised and ready. Their examination over, they removed from their bags what seemed to the photographer a bottle of black India ink.

Canning first lifted the dead man's left hand as Nicholls removed the lid from the bottle and soaked a clean white cloth in the liquid, ensuring the material was given time to soak up the substance. He then gently and with a tenderness far greater than that shown by the doctors who had last worked on the corpse, dabbed it in turn on the fingertips of Thomas Thomas. He then smoothed a sheet of white paper beneath the hand and Canning gently pressed each digit against it, leaving a small oval black smudge. The two men then carried out the same procedure on the right hand.

"Now we have his fingerprints for comparison," Nicholls said to the silent photographer.

Chapter Eight:
He intended to be late

ON THE MORNING OF Wednesday, February 16, three days after the discovery of the body, Nicholls and Canning visited Thomas Thomas' lodgings at Number Two Glanyrafon Villas to interview the two men with whom the shopkeeper spent most of what could be considered his free time. Thomas Charles Hooper Mountstephens of the Star Stores murder was 34 years of age. The son of a piano tuner, Mountstephens and his wife Lily moved to Wales some thirteen years earlier and their sons Arthur, now 12, and William, 10, were both born in the village. They had lived at their current address for eight years. Mountstephens worked at the Gellyceidrim Colliery in Glanaman, initially as a pumpman following his arrival in the village in 1908 and then as a fitter. Nicholls, in only the short time he had been in Garnant, was aware of the growing suspicion that was beginning to fall on the landlord. Mountstephens was considered distant and aloof. His ability to supplement his £8 per weekly wage with income from two lodgers only served to exacerbate the distancing of the family from the rest of Garnant's residents who struggled to make ends meet. Mountstephens' refusal to walk across the valley with Impey to ensure that all was well with the shopkeeper on the night of the murder only served to foster the ill-feeling towards him and cast a deepening shadow of suspicion over him.

During the interview, Mountstephens detailed his friendship with his former lodger and the previous manager at the Star, John Lewis, before his departure from the village in November 1919. Mountstephens believed Lewis had been transferred to another branch of the Star but was unaware where. He told the detectives how Mr Lewis had first introduced Thomas Thomas to the family, suggesting that as he was due to take over his position at the Star he might as well take his share of the bed in Glanyrafon Villas too. Mountstephens and his wife had found the new man perfectly agreeable, perhaps a little more religious and austere in his habits than his predecessor, though they considered that to be little of their business. His demeanour and nature had proved no impediment to the shopkeeper settling into life at Glanyrafon Villas and the Mountstephens family had been more than happy to accept him into their home, particularly as the situation provided a smooth and seamless transition from one paying tenant to the next.

A friendship had developed between landlord and lodger over the subsequent months and Mountstephens would regularly call into the Star when passing simply for a brief chat with Mr Thomas. He had also, on more than one Saturday evening, either arrived at the Star shortly before closing time and remained after the staff had left or gone to the shop after hours to help Mr Thomas with his end-of-day tasks, such as stock-checking, cashing up and balancing the accounts. While at Glanyrafon Villas, the two men would on occasion spend their evenings engaged in a game of chess, though the shopkeeper was no match for his more knowledgeable opponent.

On the day that Thomas Thomas was killed, Mountstephens had, with his wife and children, visited Star Stores at around 8pm, shortly before closing. During the course of a conversation with Mr Thomas, Mountstephens had inquired as to whether his lodger would be returning home late and, if so, would he like Lily to keep his supper warm. The shopkeeper confirmed that he expected to be working well into the night and would be grateful for a hot meal once he finally arrived home. Mountstephens told the detectives he had offered to return to the shop after closing – once he had safely walked his wife and children home – to assist with the tasks at hand and hasten an earlier return for the shopkeeper. However, Mr Thomas was firm in his belief that he would require no extra help that evening. He intended to spend the hours after closing making a thorough examination of the cash ledgers and accounts books and there would be no assistance that Mountstephens could offer that might hasten his return. The Mountstephens family then left the shop by the main door leading on to the valley road and walked down Coronation Arcade, past Arcade Terrace and across the fields behind to Glanyrafon Villas. Neither Mountstephens nor his wife was in the habit of using the cellar door. Nicholls noted in his pad that the family had arrived home at 8.30pm.

Neither husband nor wife left the house again that evening, apart from when Mountstephens stepped outside at 11pm to look for the lights coming from the rear of the Star Stores across the valley. He told Nicholls that once the lights were extinguished he would know Mr Thomas was making his way home and he and Lily would then wait a little longer for their lodger to join them for dinner. When he had glanced across the valley over the filling pool of mist he could clearly see the lights still burning. At 11pm – and with their young sons already asleep in bed, the husband and wife ate supper. Forty-five minutes later, Lily Mountstephens kissed her husband goodnight and went to bed. Sometime between midnight and 12.30am, Mountstephens told the detectives, he had been sitting by the hearth when he heard the sound of his second lodger, Arthur Impey, approaching up the hill. Mountstephens told the detectives he had gone outside to await him and to once more look for the lights at the rear of Commerce Place.

"Mr Impey asked what I was doing so I told him I was looking for Mr Thomas," Mountstephens explained to the Scotland Yard men. "Mr Impey suggested we walk over to the Star together to make sure everything was well. I told him he should have his supper first and then we would see. I expected that Mr Thomas would be home by then."

After eating his meal, Impey again suggested that they walk back across the valley to the Star.

"I told him that Mr Thomas had warned me that he intended to be late," Mountstephens told Nicholls.

At around 1am Thomas Mountstephens told Arthur Impey to ensure he left enough food, which was simmering in the oven, for Thomas Thomas when he finally returned and retired to bed for the night. He told the detectives that he rose between 8.30am and 9am next morning. Shortly after breakfast he had gone into the garden to feed his chickens the remnants of the previous evening's supper. He had not, at that point, yet considered the whereabouts of the shopkeeper. While he was in the garden, two young boys appeared and told him that he was urgently needed by Mr Jeffreys at the Star Stores. It was only then that he realised he had not seen the shopkeeper's boots. Mr Thomas was in the habit, when he returned home from work at the end of each day, of removing his boots and placing them just inside the kitchen door alongside Mountstephens' own footwear. The landlord had not absorbed the implication of the missing boots when he put on his own to step outside to inspect his garden and feed his foul, but with the alarm now raised, the absence grew in significance. He accompanied the boys back to the shop and was informed by Sergeant Richards of the events which occurred the previous evening. He also saw the dead body of Thomas Thomas, he told Nicholls.

"Before leaving the house I asked Mr Impey why he had not told me that Mr Thomas had not come home," he added, but he could not remember the other man's reply.

On the instructions of the Chief Constable, Mountstephens then drove by car to Mumbles on the outskirts of Swansea and collected John Thomas, the stationmaster, so that he might be at his dead brother's side and carry out the formal procedures required of the next of kin.

Nicholls and Canning then turned their attention to Arthur Impey and he too was formally interviewed. Impey told them he had arrived home shortly before midnight, coming directly from his shift at Gellyceidrim Colliery. The collier's version of the events at Number Two, Glanyrafon Villas, that evening proved relatively consistent with that of his landlord. He had lodged with the Mountstephens family since shortly after his arrival at Garnant and had remained on good terms with the couple and their children. He had enjoyed a pleasant relationship with Thomas Thomas' predecessor Mr Lewis and had grown friendly with the new shopkeeper during the past eighteen months or so of their sharing a bed. Impey said he considered himself a close friend of his landlord and the pair had been instrumental in setting up the Cwmaman Chess Club which had held its inaugural competition night the week before the murder.

However, the Londoner, whose East End accent remained as strong as ever, told the detectives that he had urged Mountstephens to walk with across the valley a second time at around 1am to ensure all was well, but the landlord had again refused, brushing off his concerns with a reminder of Mr

Thomas' plans to work late. Mountstephens went to bed but Impey had chosen to stay up and wait for his bed-mate. The longer he waited the more unlikely it seemed to him that a man of Mr Thomas' staunch convictions would choose to work so late into the Sabbath. He told Nicholls that he eventually went to bed at 4am, having convinced himself that Mr Thomas must have gone to Swansea to spend his day of rest with his brother's family and inadvertently left the lights on at the Star when he locked up. The following morning, he told the police, he had not had the opportunity to tell Mountstephens that Mr Thomas had not returned before the two boys appeared at the garden gate.

Nicholls and Canning returned to the police station to compare notes and discuss their observations of the two men. It seemed utterly remarkable to both officers that neither Mountstephens nor Impey – both of whom claimed to be as near to a close friend as the dead shopkeeper could muster – had taken any steps to check on Mr Thomas' well-being. Despite his prediction that he would be working late, neither man had ever previously known the shopkeeper to stay away from home overnight. Although he regularly stayed behind at the Star after the staff had left he had never previously remained there beyond midnight nor had he ever gone directly to visit his relatives in Swansea without alerting his landlord and bed-mate, and certainly never before at such an hour.

It was clear from his description of his movements and shift pattern at the colliery that Impey had a full and thorough explanation for his movements on the evening and night of the murder. Canning agreed to confirm with his colleagues and his employers that Impey had indeed been working the hours he had claimed on Saturday, February 12, but should those inquiries prove, as Nicholls expected them to be, confirmed, then no suspicion of the crime whatsoever could rest upon his shoulders. Thomas Mountstephens however, had no such alibi on which he could rely.

Mrs Mountstephens, when questioned by Canning, repeated her husband's version of the events of Saturday, February 12, and nothing at any stage of the investigation appeared to contradict their story. However, the two policemen were aware that confirmation of a suspect's whereabouts by his spouse alone could never be treated with the same degree of certainty as that given by an independent third party – or in Impey's case numerous third parties, including his shift supervisor and work-mates. Mountstephens had no independent witness to validate his claims with regard his movements.

By Mountstephens' own admission he had been at the Star Stores shortly before closing time and had walked down Coronation Arcade, passing close to the rear door of the Star – the means by which the killer almost certainly entered the building. There was no one – apart from Mrs Mountstephens – who could vouch for his whereabouts between the time he was last seen in the store and midnight or thereabouts when Impey arrived home. Mountstephens stated he had arrived at Glanyrafon Villas around 8.30pm, but no witness could corroborate the claim, and certainly none could confirm he had remained there, particularly after his young sons had retired for the night. Neither Thomas nor Lily Mountstephens could recall seeing any witness who might have seen them on their walk home after leaving the shop. It was also now well know in the village that both the broom handle and the knife had been found at a point directly on a line between the rear basement door of the Star Stores and Glanyrafon Villas.

It was equally obvious that Mountstephens was familiar with the internal layout of the Star and had an intimate knowledge of Thomas Thomas' methods in relation to his use of the two cash tins, the safe and his habit of returning the tins to the safe before returning to the grocery counter to total his final tallies before locking away the day's takings. Time and again during the course of their post-interview discussions, Nicholls and Canning returned to the question of why, when his lodger had not returned home at one in the morning, had Mountstephens done nothing to investigate his friend's whereabouts, and indeed why he had twice refused Impey's request to walk over to the Star. The officers were aware that there was a growing majority among the residents of Garnant who were asking the same question.

Chapter Nine:
When man turns God from his soul

DAWN WAS LATE IN COMING on the morning of Thursday, February 18. When the darkness of night finally did subside it gave way to thick black clouds swollen with freezing rain which fell with a grim incessancy throughout the day. Constable Thomas remained stationed outside the Star Stores and gave short shrift to the now only occasional gawkers who attempted to peer in beyond the drawn shutters to catch a glimpse of the murderous scene inside. Meanwhile, outside Number Two, Glanyrafon Villas, where the funeral of Thomas Thomas was due to begin, more than 300 people had gathered to pay their last respects to the slain man. Inside, the body of Thomas Thomas had already been placed in a coffin of unpolished oak with silver fittings. The sealed lid bore the inscription: Thomas Thomas, Died 12th February 1921, Aged 44 Years. No mention of the manner of his end was made on the casket, nor would it be on his headstone when he finally came to rest in the village where he had been born.

Despite the rain and sombre mood, stilted gossip and hushed rumour still raged amongst the gathered mourners as the manner of Thomas Thomas' death and the identity of the culprit remained the only topic on village lips. Some of those present poured scorn on the efforts of the men from Scotland Yard, claiming they were baffled by the crime, had come on a wasted trip and were sure to soon return to the metropolis. Others reported that a telling new clue had been uncovered that very morning and an arrest was to be made that day. Those reports, however, were wrong.

At 11am, Reverend John Thomas, pastor of Bethesda Chapel in Glanaman where Thomas Thomas had regularly gone to worship, opened the proceedings with a short private service conducted inside the house. The dead man's brother, his

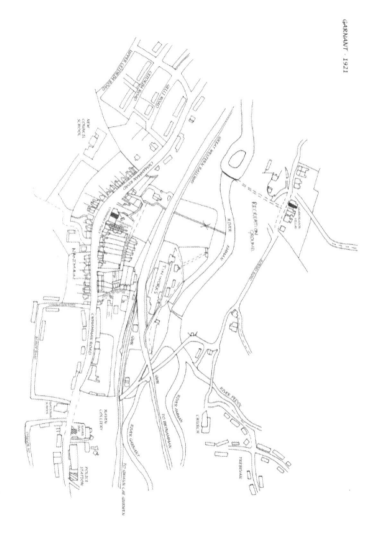

GARNANT · 1921

The sketch map of Garnant created by George Nicholls.

Commerce Place, Garnant, photographed for Scotland Yard shortly after the murder.

Inside the well-stocked Star Stores; the two counters stand on either side of the police photograph.

The police photograph of the provisions counter, from the back room.

The open safe.

The rear door of the Star Stores: was it open or locked?

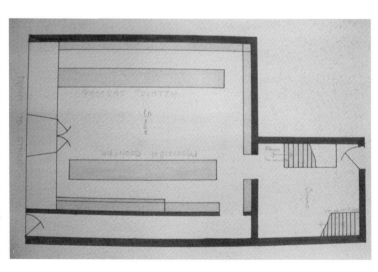

Nicholls' sketch of the floor plan of the store.

Phoebe Jones, chief assistant at the store.

Morgan Jeffreys: guilty in the eyes of many local people.

Local policeman Sergeant Richards holds the murder weapon.

George Nicholls, one of Scotland Yard's leading detectives.

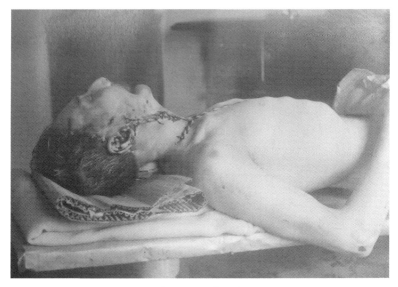

The frail body of Thomas Thomas, after the post mortem.

Thomas Morgan, chief suspect.

landlord and representatives of the Star Tea Company were the only people present. Those outside jostled and pressed as close to doors and windows as decency would allow, in a bid to hear what was being said over the coffin. Rev Thomas then moved outside to address the throng and from the shelter of the doorstep raised the spectre of the brutal crime that had brought them all to gather there.

"I believe it would be better that the murderer lay in this coffin than Mr Thomas Thomas," he told the hushed crowd. "The people of the Amman Valley will never feel more than what they do this day. No man has ever left Cwmaman under such tragic circumstances."

Then, glaring from face to face of those in the crowd and staring hard into eyes of any who dared hold his gaze, with the fire and brimstone authority he would often so often display from his pulpit, he proclaimed: "The moment man turns God out from his soul, his conscience has left him, and he has no control over life."

Of those present, few were not then moved to tears as the Reverend led them in a rendition of the miners' hymn, 'Yn y dyfroedd mawr a'r tonnau' – In the great waters and the waves. Reverend William Williams, the vicar of Garnant, also offered up a few short words in memory of the dead man, but all thoughts lingered on Rev Thomas' proclamation and the realisation that a killer without remorse walked amongst them, quite possibly right there in the midst of the gathered crowd.

At precisely 11.30am the coffin was carried from the house on the shoulders of Inspector Eardley, Councillor David Jones, Mr D Evans and Mr D Thomas, the regional inspector and respective managers of the Porthcawl, Llandovery, Ammanford and Llandeilo branches of the Star Supply Company. John Thomas, the dead man's brother, and his wife were the only family mourners present. The four shopworkers placed the coffin in the rear of the waiting motor hearse and covered it in the wreaths and floral tributes sent by the directors of the Star Supply Company in London, the staff from Star Stores branches in Ammanford, Bridgend and Carmarthen, numerous residents of Garnant and Glanaman, and one from Mr and Mrs Phillips of Bridgend, with whom Thomas Thomas had once lodged. The hearse departed at a stilted walking pace and led a slow procession of some thirty cars along the valley road where every business in Garnant and Glanaman had closed for the day in tribute and where the blinds of every house had been drawn down "as a token of the deepest sympathy" of the twin communities. The five mile road to Ammanford was thronged with people as the funeral procession made its slow progress westward to Llangendeirne churchyard for interment. In Ammanford, the streets were crowded with sympathisers as the cortege passed by, followed by the many Garnant and Glanaman residents who made the thirty mile journey to attend the burial in the dead man's home village.

Following the service, the mourners took shelter in the Farmers Arms pub across the road from the churchyard cemetery where refreshments had been arranged. While at the pub, John Thomas, stationmaster and brother of the deceased, was approached by a man he had never seen before. He did not recall seeing the man at the house in Garnant nor at the graveside, though the fellow could well have been present at both, although it was just possible that he had arrived later, after the mourners had adjourned to the Farmers Arms. The stranger appeared to be in his mid to late twenties, more than 25 but less than 30 certainly. He stood roughly five-foot-four or possibly just slightly taller, with rather small, shallow features and dark eyes. He wore a thin, unimpressive moustache. On his head was a cap pulled down, covering his hair and ears and casting a darkness about his features. His dress was otherwise unnoteworthy.

The man leant in close to John Thomas without introduction or conversation and whispered above the hubbub of pub talk: "I know who killed the shopkeeper."

John Thomas turned to look at the man, but he turned his face away so as the dead man's brother could only see him in profile.

"Thomas Mountstephens murdered your brother," he said. "He is a wicked, evil man. He cannot be trusted. He is a man of bad character."

The stranger then claimed it was well-known throughout the valley that Mountstephens was the killer. "I was surprised that your brother ever went to lodge with him – or that he stayed there," he said finally, then disappeared back amongst the bodies of the crowded bar.

John Thomas saw no reason to press the stranger on his claims or make any attempt to follow him and discover his identity. Nor did he see any reason to report the conversation to the police until two days had passed.

"He took no steps whatever to find out who this man was who was speaking to him, nor did he ask him any questions upon his statements," wrote an exasperated Nicholls in his report to Scotland Yard after finally being informed of the conversation. "He does not know whether the man was in the funeral party, where he came from or whither he went."

PART THREE

Chapter Ten:
A considerable amount of suspicion

IT WAS CLEAR TO Detective Inspector Nicholls that the murder of Thomas Thomas had been a brutal, bloody affair. It was equally clear that the brutality and the blood could and should have provided him with a clear indication of the culprit. However, the events which had taken place in and around Number Two, Commerce Place, in the days which followed the killing of the shopkeeper had left him without an obvious path to follow. By luck or by judgement, or by the interfering hands of the women of Garnant there was not a single worthwhile clue to follow. There were however two key questions which remained at the forefront of his mind.

Firstly, and seemingly most importantly to Nicholls, was the means by which the killer had gained access to the Star. The facts available presented a number of possibilities, each plausible enough based on the available evidence, though – it seemed to Nicholls – with varying degrees of likelihood. The shopkeeper could have unlocked the door and welcomed in a late arrival who came calling after the closure of the store for the night. Thomas was well-known to be a dedicated company man and the thought of a few extra shillings in the till would most likely have seen him happy to bolster his day's takings, particularly if he recognised the customer as a regular or familiar face around the village who wanted nothing more than a box of tea or a few ounces of butter. There was also the possibility that the killer had entered the store unnoticed through the back cellar door shortly after closing time when Nellie Richards had run next door to the home of Mrs Jeffreys to ask about the state of Phoebe Jones' dress. The premise, however, seemed the least likely to the detective's thinking. The girl had been gone no more than a few minutes and would have left the killer with just the narrowest window of opportunity to enter. He, for Nicholls was in no doubt that the killer was man, would have had to come through the door – which had been left ajar rather than wide open, completely unaware of what lay behind it, whether one of the shop-boys, Miss Jones or even Thomas Thomas himself, might have spotted his entry. The scenario of a passing thief noticing the open door just as the girl Richards left and taking his chance to enter the shop in the hope of hiding in the basement until the other staff had left to then steal whatever he might find, appeared too coincidental, too random and too opportunistic for a man of Nicholls' thinking. He was however all too aware that men had been killed for far less than a pat of butter or a tin of strawberry jam, and far too experienced to rule out such a possibility altogether. The scenario, he did admit to himself, would and could become more plausible with one slight variation: what if it had not been mere coincidence that the killer was lurking hidden in the shadows at the rear of the Star when Nellie Richards carried out her errand? Such a scenario led inevitably to one conclusion, that the killer had expected Nellie – or some other member of staff – to leave by the back door at the time she did. As Nellie had been the only member of staff to leave the store at anywhere near that time the question had to be asked whether she might have had some involvement, perhaps leaving the door ajar for her lover to get in. The thought seemed implausible. A second more realistic possibility would involve the person who had sent Nellie on her errand. Phoebe Jones was a far more likely suspect than the teenager. She had, after all, been the one to send Nellie on her errand. She was also older and seemingly more likely to have had a lover capable of such a crime. Left alone with the shopkeeper after the more junior staff had departed for the night she would have had far greater opportunity to ensure the crime was carried out. Nicholls was aware that there were occasional rumours that Miss Jones was under suspicion. However, he felt that to have carried out the crime was beyond her. To have gone to the dance while a lover or accomplice carried out the brutal crime would have required a degree of calculated evil he could not associate with the shop assistant. He was aware of the dangers of underestimating a woman having come to Wales fresh from his involvement in the Bamberger case, but Lily Amelia Taylor seemed a wholly different animal to the timid Welsh shopworker. He could not believe that the woman who had gone out to see if she might peer through blinds, who had tried to rouse Mr Jeffreys from his bed, who had screamed at the discovery of the body, was the cold-blooded mastermind behind such a crime.

The third, and it seemed to Nicholls most likely, scenario was one in which the killer had gone into the store with at least robbery on his mind. Customers were welcome to make their own way to the basement and choose a suitable box with which to carry home their purchases throughout the cellar door. Nicholls could well imagine the culprit entering the Star a short time before closing and making his way downstairs without drawing any great attention to himself. Then, when out of sight of staff or other customers, slipping unseen into some darkened corner to bide his time and wait until only the frail, deaf shopkeeper remained. A second possibility, which followed a similar track, would see someone entering the shop and leaving via the cellar door and realising as they walked away how easy it would be to return and slip inside unnoticed.

Such a course raised numerous new questions, particularly in terms of the nature of the killer. If Nicholls' thinking was correct, it seemed unlikely the culprit would have lurked so long in the dust and cobwebs for little more than a armful of tinned food. It seemed almost certain to Nicholls that the crime had not been committed as a theft of opportunity, but that the killer had entered the store with an eye on the weekend's takings. Perhaps he had been aware of Thomas Thomas' habit of counting the money on the provisions counter and placing the two tins in the safe, leaving the steel box open to return to the shop for his receipt books. Perhaps the killer had hoped he might be able to take his chance and grab the money boxes during that brief moment. More likely was the thought that the thief had planned to confront the frail shopkeeper, safe in the knowledge that Thomas Thomas' health and physique would have offered little resistance to physical aggression, no matter how willing and determined he might be to put up a fight.

The second fundamental question in Nicholls' mind rested on the injuries sustained by the dead man. Dr Jones had been absolutely certain that each of the three injuries – the brutal blows to the head, the stab to the abdomen and the knife wound to the throat – was serious enough to have proved fatal in their own right. Each would have led to Thomas Thomas' certain death, alone and helpless behind the shop counter overnight. The critical detail however would surely have been how quickly each wound might have taken to end the dying man's life – and therefore, perhaps most importantly, in which order they had been struck.

Dr Jones had appeared to grow ever more confident in his timing of those dreadful minutes: the blow to the head followed by the stab to the stomach and then finally and most fatally, the plunging of the blade into Thomas Thomas' neck. The doctor's view appeared to illustrate an attack growing ever more frenzied with each passing minute and each subsequent strike; an attacker who perhaps had not intended to kill, but who found themselves in a situation spiralling out of control and beyond all possibility of recall. Based on the available information, the doctor's evaluation made sense. Furthermore, and coupled with the initial description of the scene presented to Nicholls, the layout of the Star Stores and the final resting place of Thomas Thomas' body, it also appeared to offer the detective his only solid, albeit limited, clue. For the wounds to have been caused in the order that the doctor described, the killer must have been right-handed. It would have been impossible for a left-handed person to have swung the broom with enough force to have felled any man, even one of Thomas Thomas' frail disposition. The doorway between the storeroom at the top of the stairs and the shop meant such a blow could not have been struck there while the walls and shelves behind the provisions counter would have made it impossible for a left-handed man to swing the broom at all. The doctor's assessment of the injuries ensured that only a right-handed man could have used the broom, with the full scope of the shop's interior, to strike a blow with enough force and momentum to inflict such deadly injury.

However, despite the credibility of Doctor Jones' assessment of events, there remained a flicker of doubt in the mind of the man from Scotland Yard regarding such absolute certainty. Initially, the doctor had been unwilling to speculate on the order of the injuries suffered by the dead man. Indeed, his early interview with Sergeant Richards had been marked by a definite refusal to predict the time-line of the attack. That lack of certainty had disappeared by the time of the conversation with the man from the local press and once having been quoted in the newspaper, Dr Jones appeared unwilling to change his opinion. The interview with the pressman may have occurred after the doctor had at last reached a firm conclusion despite taking place prior to the post-mortem examination, but equally the physician might have found himself forming his opinion only after he had read his own words in the local paper and found himself in the awkward position of feeling unable to cast doubt on his own professional reasoning once it had been made public. Nicholls could not escape the nagging doubt however, and he found himself questioning whether it might be possible to cause such extreme and repeated damage to the human skull with nothing more deadly than a broom while a man remained standing, or even once he was helpless lying on the floor.

The cleansing of all trace of evidence had denied Nicholls the opportunity to form his own opinion. He would never know what conclusion he might have drawn from bloodstains, overturned furniture and the inevitable marks and scuffs left when two men come together had he been able to experience the true aftermath at the heart of Star Stores. The true horror of the events of February 12 had forever been erased by soap suds and scrubbing brushes long before his arrival in West Wales.

Thomas Mountstephens remained the prime suspect amongst the valley gossips – and also, it was becoming abundantly clear to Nicholls, those less willing to indulge in idle chit-chat. "Quite early in the investigation the suggestion was made that Mr Thomas Mountstephens was thoroughly acquainted with the methods employed by the deceased man and it was pointed out that the spot where the weapons were found in the brook was in a line with the direction which would be taken by a person coming from the back of the Star Stores and going to Mr Mountstephens' house," noted Nicholls. "There has been raised a considerable amount of suspicion and feeling against him in Garnant."

Despite also harbouring his suspicions towards the dead man's landlord – most notably due to his at best indifference, at worst unwillingness to walk back to the Star with Impey – Nicholls was keen to ensure he did not become too focused on one man and in doing so allow the real culprit to escape detection. The suspicions surrounding Morgan Jeffreys also seemed little more than gossip to Nicholls' mind. Despite the former butcher's reputation as a powerful man, it was clear that Morgan was not as fit and healthy as he once had been.

With the help of Canning and Sergeant Richards, Nicholls continued to pursue every lead and suspicion presented to him, however tenuous. Most proved little more than simple tasks of elimination, but two men in particular, though outside any obvious involvement at the Star Stores, remained high on his list of those to whom 'interest attaches'. While the majority of Garnant residents remained keen to point the finger of suspicion on an outsider – and particularly the Londoner Mountstephens, there were some – Police Sergeant Richards included – who believed the culprit might have had his origins closer to home.

The first, and most obvious person of interest, was a known convict named David Lewis. Lewis was, officially at least, a resident of nearby Gwaun cae Gurwen, just a few of miles east along the valley road. He had served at least three terms of hard labour at Brecon Prison, with sentences ranging from six or nine months for theft and larceny. Following his latest period of incarceration, Lewis had been released with a duty to report weekly to Gwaun cae Gurwen police station, but had failed to do so for 'a considerable time'. Lewis was technically on the run and had not been seen in the valley for a number of years. While his criminal record and history of theft and – on occasion – violence ensured he would remain a suspect until proved otherwise, the fact he could not possibly have known the habits of Thomas Thomas made him an unlikely fit for the crime. Nicholls accepted it was possible Lewis has returned unnoticed by the authorities to the valley in recent days and, by chance, been at the rear of the Star when the cellar door was left open, but it seemed most improbable. The fact Lewis was a man of at least 65 years also seemed, to Nicholls mind, to further reduce the likelihood that he might have been able enter the rear of the shop by chance and unnoticed when the opportunity had presented itself. Nevertheless, Nicholls refused to rule him out of the investigation without giving him further consideration.

A second man upon whom some considerable interest was attached lived much more locally than Lewis – and was certainly in the village on the night of Saturday, February 12. He was also known to have been in the Star Stores on the day in question. His name was Thomas Conway Hewitt Morgan. Morgan lived with his wife at a rented property less than a mile from Star Stores just off the valley road between the junctions of Horney Road and Old Station Road. Morgan was a relatively regular customer at the Star and, like Lewis, a convicted criminal. Sergeant Richards had informed Nicholls soon after his arrival in Garnant that the man known as Tom Morgan was high on his personal list of suspects. "A man upon whom strong local suspicion of the crime falls is Thomas Conway Hewitt Morgan," noted Nicholls in his report back to Scotland Yard.

Morgan was 28 years of age and his reputation as an untrustworthy individual of low moral standards and dubious character was widespread throughout the Amman Valley. He stood five-feet-five tall, had a disfigured right hand and walked with a limp. He was also a man well known to both Sergeant Richards and PC Thomas. Morgan was said to have been in the Star either in the late afternoon or early evening of February 12. Phoebe Jones had, in her statement, mentioned his presence and, though she had recalled seeing "the man with the crippled hand" enter the store, she had no recollection of seeing him leave. The assumption had been that he, like many other customers, he had gone into the basement and left through the rear door. Morgan Jeffreys also claimed he had seen Morgan hanging around the entrance to the Arcade, both on the day of the murder and on several occasions during the month leading up to the bloody crime.

Originally from Llandovery where his grandfather – a watchmaker – had been a gentleman of some standing and had designed and built the clock in the tower of the town hall, Morgan had settled in Garnant in 1917 after marrying Ethel Clark, a shop assistant in Ammanford. While David Morgan had been considered a gentleman of the town, his son Evan had fallen in the eyes of the community and was – by the time of Tom's birth – working as a travelling tailor, moving from one South Wales community to another. If working as an itinerant needlesmith was deemed something of a come-down for the Morgan family, the depths to which young Tom dragged the family name was a source of perpetual shame.

Thomas Conway Euard Morgan was born on September 15, 1892, in the hamlet of Llangadock near Llandovery. His birth was registered on October 22 of the same year. His name however was to prove as flexible as his father's employment. By the time of the 1901 census, his parents were recording his third initial as an H, and for the remainder of his life he would regularly slip between Thomas Conway Euard Morgan, Thomas Conway Euart Morgan, Thomas Conway Hewitt Morgan, a simple Thomas or Tom Morgan and Conway Morgan as the mood – or need – required. From early in his youth, Tom had developed a reputation as one with little regard for the nuanced differences between right and wrong. From childhood, he was well known to the officers of the law and his first appearance before a court came in Llandovery on January 16, 1904, when he was bound over after admitting petty larceny in relation to the theft of three boxes of chocolates and three shillings from a shop in the town. Tom was 11 years old, but the fearful and intimidating environs of the courthouse did little to change his nature. Bound over he may have been, but Tom remained indifferent to the law and the notion of personal property. Precisely six years and one day on from his first appearance before the magistrates, Tom Morgan was again brought before the court. This time however he would not be treated so leniently. On January 17, 1910, he was found guilty of housebreaking, burglary and theft.

The Carmarthenshire Quarterly Assizes Court was told how Mr James Rees James of Llandovery and his wife had chosen to spend the Christmas holiday in London with relatives. The couple had departed Llandovery on December 20, leaving their home in the care of their trusted housekeeper, who, though she did not live on the premises, would make daily visits to ensure the fires remained alight. Upon their return on January 5, Mr and Mrs James discovered they had been burgled. The thief had made off with a guinea, a silver match box, a silver pen, a magnifying glass and a pair of gold cuff links belonging to Mr James. He had also taken numerous items of jewellery belonging to Mrs James. The goods stolen had a combined worth of £18, approaching one month's wages for a married man with children to feed. Most devious of all, the thief had avoided the rooms which the housekeeper would visit on her daily check, ensuring the act would go unnoticed until the James family returned. It was clear to the court that the burglary had not been an opportunist crime, but had been well planned with the house-keeper's movements noted.

At the time of the burglary, Tom Morgan was fifteen and had been working as a collier in Llandybie – a short distance from Ammanford. However, like the James family, Tom had spent Christmas visiting relations, namely his parents in Llandovery. The town police had wasted little time in concluding that the return of Tom Morgan and the burglary at the James home were no coincidence. Officers visited Evan Morgan's home where young Tom was staying and discovered the majority of the haul hidden in Tom's room. A smart burglar young Tom may have been but a clever criminal he was not, and he had little choice but to admit his guilt.

When Tom was brought before the grand jury of the Assizes, Sergeant James Deans of Llandovery Police was asked to offer some insight into the youth the local press had been quick to dub 'the boy burglar'. Deans said he had known Tom for more than seven years, his first involvement with the boy coming when Tom was just eight – three years before his conviction for the theft of the chocolates.

"Is his character good?" the Judge, Lord Justice Coleridge asked.

"No, it is not my Lord," replied the sergeant.

The guilty plea for the crime of house burglary was enough for the court to reach its conclusion and further charges relating to the burglary of the town's Market Hall, alleged to have taken place the day after the house raid, were dropped due to insufficient evidence. Due to his poor character, the planning behind the crime and his previous conviction, the Judge ordered that 15-year-old Thomas Morgan be incarcerated. Due to his age, his guilty plea and the fact that many of the stolen items were recovered, Tom escaped hard labour and was instead sent to spend twelve months in a Borstal institution.

In 1908, the newly-enacted Prevention of Crime Act looked

to expand the use of a model institution designed to rehabilitate young offenders. In 1902 a programme had been introduced with the goal of keeping young offenders separate from more seasoned adult criminals. It was hoped that by introducing the specific institutions for young offenders they might be steered off the path towards a lifetime of criminality at an early age. The first such institution was created in the village of Borstal near Rochester in Kent. The regime, though strict and highly regulated was aimed at educating the young interns rather than merely punishing them for the previous illegal acts. Based on a military regime, there was a focus on routine, discipline and authority. Borstal was deemed a success and the 1908 act saw the creation of a series of new institutions all over the country based on the model.

Tom Morgan was released from the institution on January 16, 1911, and remained under supervision until July 16 of that year. As with many of the boys who had been sent to such institutions, Tom was encouraged to join the army following his release and period of supervision and on May 17, 1912, at the Tumble recruitment office he was passed as fit and able for duty. He enlisted in the 4th Battalion the Welsh Regiment.

With the Great War well under way and the Welsh Regiments about to embark for the trenches of Flanders, Tom Morgan was invalided out of the army having been declared unfit for active service on April 26, 1915. With many of the young men of the valley signing up to fight for King and Country, Tom Morgan – a soldier with almost three years in uniform to his name – returned home having been declared lame with a diagnosis of ankylosis of the big toe and second toe of his left foot. Ankylosis is a stiffness or rigidity of the joint, most likely caused by some prior injury.

On September 30, 1915, Tom Morgan married in the Ammanford registry office. At 33, Ethel Clark, who hailed from Newport in Gwent, was a little over eleven years the senior of her new husband. The couple initially lived in Ammanford, but moved to Garnant within two years of their marriage – taking up the tenancy of Old Anchor House – no more than 15 minutes walk from Star Stores. Despite his status as a former soldier, Tom could not escape his past and his reputation as 'the boy burglar' remained – and so too did the distrust with which he was held in the valley, which seemed to grow with each passing year. After leaving the army and following his wedding, Tom initially returned to the only form of reputable employment he had known and took up posts at a number of local collieries. Mining remained back-breaking work during the war years with colliers deep underground hacking away at the coal-face, each filling their tram with black treasure before it was hauled back to the surface. As a means of ensuring each man earned his weekly wage, the miners would mark their full tram with their number before sending it back above ground. Tom Morgan earned himself a reputation – and the hatred of the men underground – for intercepting trams on the way back to the surface and replacing the rightful owner's chalked number with his own. He found himself dismissed from a number of the valley collieries, including Raven and Gellyceidrim for the offence. Soon he found he was not welcome at any of the collieries in the Amman valley.

Sergeant Richards told Nicholls that Morgan had, since his arrival in the village, also been suspected of numerous thefts and burglaries though none had ever mustered enough evidence to support a prosecution. "It is not surprising that suspicion in connection with the present crime should fall upon him," Nicholls noted.

However, no matter how black his reputation and formidable his criminal record, one piece of evidence conclusively eliminated Morgan from any list of potential suspects in relation to the killing of Thomas Thomas at Star Stores. While the vital piece of information had been withheld from the press, Dr Jones remained adamant that the killer had struck the fatal blows in the order of the strike to the head, followed by the stab to the abdomen and then the stab to the neck. For the wounds to have occurred in such an order, the killer must have attacked the shop keeper with the broom in his right hand. There could, according to the doctor's thesis, be no other possibility.

Such medical conviction completely ruled out all possibility that Thomas Conway Hewitt Morgan might be the killer. In June, 1920, lame Tom Morgan had been the victim of a bizarre and still unexplained accident. According to Sergeant Richards, Morgan had been out one night with his younger brother David, who also lived in the village. The two men had been "in a field late at night not far distant from the Railway Station, and the Garnant Tin Works". While, according to the brothers, innocently walking through the field in the dead of night, an explosion tore off the thumb and index, middle and ring finger of Tom Morgan's right hand. Despite his brother suffering awful injuries, David did not call a doctor or the police. Instead he went to Tom Morgan's house. It was only days later, when Sergeant Richards, upon hearing of the strange tale, went to visit Morgan that any explanation was forthcoming. Morgan claimed that as he and his brother has been walking home, they had spotted "something smoking in the hedgerow". Tom went to investigate, reaching in amongst the bushes and pulling out whatever contraption it was that he found there. With the smoking item still in his hand, it exploded, ripping off his thumb and three fingers and making his right hand permanently useless.

"The local police regard this as extremely suspicious," Nicholls noted in his report, "and it does indeed seem rather weak. It seems far more likely that some explosive which Tom Morgan was carrying went off in his hand."

Nicholls and Richards were well aware that explosives were often used when poaching salmon and trout, but with the River Amman black with coal and the once bountiful stocks long since disappeared it seemed unlikely that the brothers had been out at night in search of fish. The question of what other use the Morgan men might have had for explosives was never answered and while no one believed the story of the smoking bush, there was no evidence with which Sergeant Richards might disprove it. With his right hand reduced to just his little finger, Morgan could find no work in the collieries even if they had been open to him. His reputation ensured no other business would see fit to employ him either.

"Since the date of this occurrence Tom Morgan has done no work on account of his injuries," wrote Nicholls.

In the second week of January, a little under a month before the murder, Tom Morgan has been spoken to by Sergeant Richards and PC Thomas following reports that he had been seen lurking to the rear of Commerce Place, on the rough land at the back of Star Stores. Morgan Jeffreys had summoned the police fearing that the injured man had been there to steal one of his chickens. A number of his birds had disappeared over the previous few months and Jeffreys – and the police – believed that Morgan was the culprit. Morgan and Anne Jeffreys both claimed they had seen Tom Morgan at the bottom of Coronation Arcade close to the rear of Star Stores on the afternoon of Saturday, February 12, six or seven hours before the killing of the shopkeeper, though that in itself offered no indication of any involvement in the crime. Despite the doctor's professional medical opinion that it was simply not possible for Morgan to have committed the murder, Nicholls felt Sergeant Richards' opinion was worthy of serious consideration and asked PC Thomas to visit Morgan and invite him to attend the station for an interview. "There was nothing more tangible to connect him with the crime than his bad antecedents and his appearances about the Arcade, but it was decided to call upon him to account for his movements on the day of the murder," Nicholls reported back to Scotland Yard.

On the morning of Friday, February 18, PC Thomas went to Old Anchor House with a request that Tom Morgan attend the station and – a short time later – the man with a limp and one mangled hand presented himself before the officers from New Scotland Yard. Morgan arrived dressed smartly in shirt, tie and jacket, looking more like a man attending chapel than a police station. His habit of slouching to his left – presumably because of the lameness in his left foot – seemed to trim at least two or three inches from his overall height, though Nicholls was unsure whether it was genuine or added for his benefit. Morgan wore his dark hair oiled and swept back over his head, exposing a large forehead and dark shadowy eyes. His handsome, boyish looks gave him the appearance of one only recently out of his teens rather than a man with three years in the army and 12 months incarcerated in a government institution. He was of medium build and, despite his injuries, appeared of good health and general physique. He carried himself as a person aware of his appealing looks and confident in his intellect.

With Canning taking notes, Nicholls began by asking Morgan of his current situation and his means. Morgan described his life as a married man with no children. His total income was limited to the 15 shillings he received each week under the National Health Insurance Scheme paid to him in the wake of his hand injury. The rent on Old Anchor House came to 18 shillings per calendar month leaving Morgan a little over two pounds a month to live on. Even a farm labourer could expect to earn around four pounds a week – a miner more than five. The truth was that Morgan, even long before his injury, had been dependant on his wife for an income to keep the roof over their heads. Ethel, since the days when Morgan had begun courting her prior to the outbreak of the war, had worked as a counter assistant with Mr John Wilde at his confectionary and grocery shop in Ammanford. Morgan meanwhile, spent his days "walking about the village". He was also a regular fixture at the billiard saloons in Ammanford, Gwaun cae Gurwen and Brynaman.

Morgan said he had spent the morning of February 12 with his brother David playing billiards. At lunch-time he took a stroll through the village and called into Coronation Arcade though could not recall whether he entered any of the shops either in the Arcade or in Commerce Place. He then returned to his house in the early afternoon and remained there for some time before catching the bus to Ammanford where he visited Wilde's green-grocery. After a short conversation with his wife who was serving behind the counter he caught the bus back along the valley road with the intention of visiting the Gwaun cae Gurwen Public Hall. However, realising he was late for whatever appointment he had arranged at the hall, he chose instead to depart the bus in Garnant and go home. It was 7pm or shortly after. Upon arriving home he found there was no milk in the house and called on his neighbour Mrs Williams to borrow a jug of milk. He also went to the chip shop almost directly opposite his home where he bought a bag of fried potatoes. He returned home to eat his chips with a cup of milky tea. At 8pm or shortly after, he took a slow walk through the village as far as Gellyceidrim Colliery without any real purpose other than to fill the time. Upon reaching colliery he turned and ambled once more back to his house, arriving shortly before his wife. When Ethel Morgan descended from the bus a little after 9pm, she stopped off at the frying shop and bought home two bags of chipped potatoes, one each for her husband and herself. The couple ate their supper together and remained at home for the remainder of the evening before climbing into bed at 11pm. Neither left the house after Ethel arrived home. Morgan told the detectives he was only made aware of the incident at the Star Stores on the Sunday morning when his wife informed him of the robbery and murder. Ethel, he believed, had been told of the crime by Mrs Williams, the woman who had given him the milk the previous evening.

During the course of the conversation Nicholls used the considerable skills he had developed during a career interviewing the criminals of London, Paris and Berlin in a bid to test the veracity of Morgan's story. The inspector returned the topic on a number of occasions to the injuries sustained by Morgan to his hand and foot, but on no occasion did the man sitting opposite veer from the versions of events Sergeant Nicholls had recounted. Nicholls also looked to find some chink of light in the story of Morgan's life which echoed in the village gossip. Clearly assuming that the great detective from the metropolis would have no clue as to the lives of the inhabitants of a little Welsh mining village, Morgan seemed to enjoy toying with his questioner. Nicholls let his quarry run, hoping he might trip himself. Time and again during the course of the conversation Morgan portrayed himself as a law-abiding citizen, denying any previous involvement with the police or the justice system. "He failed to mention anything about his detention in the Borstal Institute," Nicholls reported back to his commanding officer.

Eventually, when enough line had spun out from his reel, Nicholls made casual reference to the records of juvenile criminals – and only then did for the briefest of moments did Morgan's air of calm slip. Realising he had been played by the policeman, he came clean about his youthful waywardness and indiscretions. Believing himself to still have an opportunity to reclaim control of the situation, he saw his chance to confess his period of incarceration before the detective slammed it in his face. He admitted he had spent twelve months in Borstal, but dismissed it as teenage foolishness. Believing he had called the Scotland Yard man's bluff in coming clean, his calm demeanour returned and he assured Nicholls that the crime committed by 'the boy burglar' was one foolhardy act, long past and nothing more than an embarrassment to his adult maturity. However, the bluff was not complete and the game not over. Nicholls allowed Morgan to show his hand while keeping his own cards close to his chest. "He declared that that was the only occasion he had been in trouble and in that he was not telling the truth," he noted.

Wholly dissatisfied by Morgan's portrayal of a blameless adult life, Nicholls was unwilling to allow the one-handed man the opportunity to cover any tracks which might lead him back to the grisly events at Star Stores. While the ladies of Garnant had inadvertently done their utmost to hamper the investigation by cleaning the scene of the crime, Nicholls knew that there was one thing the mops and brushes of the village women had failed to scrub clean. They had forced their way past PC Thomas on the grounds that the quantity of blood spilled about the shop was an abomination. With such an excess of that vital fluid shed during the course of the crime, it was clear to such an experienced detective that the clothes of the killer would have been saturated to the point where no amount of scrubbing on the washboard would cleanse them of the traces of the deed. It was with no little surprise to Nicholls then that Tom Morgan appeared more than happy to be accompanied back to his home by Sergeant Canning.

Before their departure, Nicholls took his colleague to one side and instructed him to interview Ethel Morgan to see if he could find any schism between her version of the events of Saturday night and that of her husband. Nicholls also wanted to know more about Morgan's lifestyle and his personal finances. Most of all however, he told Canning to examine every single item of clothing in the house.

When Canning arrived back the station he detailed his conversation with Ethel Morgan. Nicholls was disappointed to learn that her story mirrored that of her husband exactly. Mrs Morgan also described her husband's daily wanderings through the village, filling his time following the injury which left him unable to secure employment – she though made no mention of his reputation as one unworthy of his colleagues' trust or of his criminal record. Canning asked about the household finances and was surprised when she produced a Post Office savings book which showed an account containing more than £80, more than Morgan would receive in six months through the National Insurance Health Scheme and far in excess what even the most thrifty shop assistant might hope to salt away. The book showed deposits of various sums over a period dating back across the past three years. The couple claimed their savings had been amassed while Morgan was employed at the colliery and had remained intact by virtue of his wife's scrupulous management of the household budget. Nicholls, when told of the account later, felt it most unlikely that a man such as Morgan, who spent his time in the billiard hall and pub, might manage to live so frugally with such a sum at his disposal. Ethel Morgan, Nicholls noted, must have kept the savings book well out of her husband's reach.

Canning's request that Mrs Morgan provide him with every item of her husband's clothing was met without resistance and the detective examined each in turn, shirts, vests and trousers.

"Nothing in the nature of any stains was found upon them," recorded Nicholls.

Canning was also aware of the piece of broken button found in the mortise of the safe door at Star Stores and he inspected each garment closely, looking for a broken or un-matching button which might have been replaced in the meantime. Again the examination was in vain. "All the buttons on Morgan's clothing were whole," recorded Nicholls.

Later that evening, while Nicholls and Canning discussed their respective interviews of Tom and Ethel Morgan, and the discoveries – and lack of them – which came from the events earlier in the day it appeared, at last, that a breakthrough may have occurred. Nicholls believed that the discovery of the murderer's blood-soaked clothing might now prove vital in their quest to find the killer. His optimistic hopes that the crucial evidence might have been uncovered on Canning's visit to Old Anchor House had been dashed, but with hopes beginning to fade the sound of the police station telephone brought an unexpected turn.

Chapter Eleven:
Willing and desirous

ON THE MORNING OF Saturday, February 19, Nicholls, Canning and PC David Thomas made their way west along the valley road to the village of Cwmtwrch in the Swansea Valley. The eight-mile journey took them out of Carmarthenshire and into the county of Glamorgan. The phone call from police station in Ystradgynlais the previous evening had caused Nicholls frustration and elation in equal measure. He was aware that the move into Glamorgan had seen the officers cross from the jurisdiction of the Carmarthenshire police into that of the Brecon Constabulary, and he was all too familiar with the jealousies and rivalries of neighbouring forces. His beloved Metropolitan police was riddled with such rivalries amid its various divisions and he had no doubt that such problems were also present between the rural constabularies. He knew that in many situations such an enmity could be good for the Force as the divisional chiefs jockeyed for position in the eyes of those above them in the only way they could, through results and cases successfully concluded. However, he had also experienced situations where arrests had been delayed – and in certain cases – investigations floundered, because one division or constabulary had failed to share information in the hope that they might claim the credit for the arrest of some villain guilty of crimes across the border. As the three men made their way to Ystradgynlais police station, Nicholls wondered whether the Brecon Constabulary was guilty of just such a tactic.

The call, which was taken by Sergeant Richards from his counterpart in the Swansea Valley, was to inform the men from Scotland Yard that items of bloodied clothing had been found hidden in a wood close to Betting Colliery. In addition to the bloodstains, the items appeared to have been marked with the initials of their owner. The discovery could, thought Nicholls, have proved the vital breakthrough in the case. For the first time there appeared – should the clothing be related to the crime – evidence which had remained untouched, or at least unsullied, by some well-meaning member of the public. However, Nicholls would struggle to hide his annoyance that despite the fact that he was hunting a killer, the officers of the Brecon Constabulary had chosen not to inform him of the find until three full days after its discovery.

The clothing – a shirt and a pair of trousers – had been found by a 33-year-old ostler named Frank Luscombe on the morning of February 15. Luscombe, a Devonian who like so many others had moved to the South Wales valleys in search of work, was responsible for tending the pit ponies as well as other general labouring tasks at the Betting Colliery, and had come across the blood-stained clothing in the woods. Following a brief discussion with the officers at Ystradgynlais, Nicholls sent Canning and Thomas – accompanied by an officer of the Brecon Constabulary – up to the colliery to search the area. They were also tasked with interviewing Luscombe and any other workers who may have witnessed anything on the 15th. Nicholls meanwhile, remained at the station to carry out a forensic examination of the clothing. The detective's initial hopes that the clothing might prove the key piece of evidence in the killing of Thomas Thomas soon began to fade.

The shirt was made of cotton with green and brown horizontal stripes running down its front and back. Inside the neckband handwritten in black ink were the initials BE. The trousers were dark in colour with a large patch of dark striped material on the right knee. There was a second, smaller patch on the left knee. There were two further patches on the seat. The patches were all of the same material and hand been hand-sewn in a purely functional fashion without any great artistry or skill. Both legs were extremely well worn and faded yellow from the knee downwards. The black buttons on the trousers bore the brand-name 'Excelsior Quality'. There were two side pockets and one hip pocket on the trousers. In the left side pocket was a small patch of blood and there were two small spots of blood near the bottom of the right leg and one on the back of the left. There was no blood on the shirt.

It was clear to Nicholls that the clothing was very old and dirty. His first thought was that the items were those which might have been worn by a tramp or itinerant beggar. The bloodstains certainly did not appear recent and, to Nicholls' experienced eye, almost certainly dated from long before the murder of the shopkeeper seven days earlier. There was also far too little blood for the wearer of the garments to have been present at the time of the frenzied killing of Thomas Thomas. Nonetheless, the detective took the clothing and on his return to Garnant would hand the items to Sergeant Richards for secure storage should they be required at some later date in the investigation. The Scotland Yard man however felt the items bore no relation to the Star Stores crime and simply ordered they be stored in line with standard Metropolitan Police procedure.

On his arrival back in the village, Nicholls discovered the village in a state of high activity. At 1.30pm a fire had broken out in the drapers shop belonging to Edward Lewis at Tydfil House just a few doors along the valley road from Commerce Place and the Star. The blaze had been discovered by Edward's wife Hannah, who immediately raised the alarm. A fire extinguisher was brought from the garage opposite along with another from the tinplate works and all those who were able chained buckets of water to scene in a bid to control the flames. With Sergeant Richards directing the operation, the fire was eventually brought under control without further damage to nearby buildings. The drapers shop was not so fortunate. The building was completely destroyed along with the rooms above where the couple lived. Stock worth hundreds of pounds had also been lost in the flames. There was no obvious cause to the blaze, which had started in the shop itself, as the fire had begun when Mr and Mrs Edwards were upstairs having their lunch break. Before even the flames had been fully extinguished the gossip mill had begun to turn. The close proximity of the drapers shop to the Star meant very few in the village saw the blaze as a coincidence. By the time dusk was falling on the valley, the over-riding view was that some vital piece of evidence – most likely the killer's bloodied clothes – had been hidden in the shop. It seemed conceivable that rather than risk attempting to recover them or face the possibility that they might be discovered by the draper or his wife, the killer had set fire to the building, destroying the evidence along with everything else inside.

The return of Canning and Thomas from Ystradgynlais took Nicholls away from the scene of the blaze. It was clear enough that nothing useful would be found in the charred remains. Back at the station, the detective sergeant briefed his superior on the day's enquiries but his information only served to reinforce Nicholls' view that the morning had been wasted. Canning had interviewed Luscombe and had found no reason to doubt his account of the discovery. Luscombe – along with other workers at Betting Colliery – had described seeing two men in the woods and around the colliery boiler house on Sunday, February 13. The men, who appeared to have no relation to one another and were never seen together, were seen at various times spotted sheltering near the boiler house on the Sunday morning. The descriptions of them were vague and varied enough to give the impression that the various witnesses were describing two differ-ent men although Canning remained unsure whether the different colliery workers had simply seen the same man at different times.

"It is not unusual for men to be allowed to sleep in the colliery boiler house," Canning reported. It seemed that provided nothing was taken, no damage caused, or the mine managers given any reason to do otherwise, a blind eye was turned to men, who were invariably tramps and the like. Such men with nowhere else to go would occasionally seek the shelter and warmth of the boiler house, particularly at the time of year when night-time temperatures fell well below freezing and thermometers were only just nudging into single figures during the hours of daylight. Such was the regularity of these unofficial visits during the winter months that the colliery workers paid the men little heed, particularly as they usually did their best to stay out of sight. None of the workers who could recall seeing the man or men on Sunday morning thought their actions unusual, none had seemed particularly suspicious or attempted to hide any more or any less than previous visitors. They had kept out of sight, yes, but it seemed to all who saw them that their efforts to remain in the shadows were more in fear of losing a warm place to sleep for the night than to escape the law for some greater crime. It was clear that by the time Canning had searched the boiler house, whoever had been sleeping there a week earlier was long gone. He would pass on the vague descriptions he had been given to the Ystradgynlais sergeant in the hope that the men might be traced in the coming days, but that hope was as flimsy as the descriptions provided of the men themselves.

Luscombe had led Canning, Thomas and local officer to the spot where he had discovered the clothing and a thorough search of the area was carried out, but found nothing further. Nor was there anything obvious which might link the items to the men or man who had slept in the boiler house that weekend. After being briefed by his sergeant and PC Thomas, Nicholls was left in little doubt that the clothing and the men at the boiler house bore no connection to the Star killing. He did however contact the local newspapers in the vague hope that he might be proved wrong and these tramps could be traced, at least in the hope of eliminating them from the investigation. The *Amman Valley Chronicle*, the *South Wales Evening Post*, the *Carmarthen Journal*, the *Cambria Daily Leader*, *South Wales News* and the *Western Mail* – all of which had been carrying detailed reports on the investigation – were sent a description of the clothing with a request that they might publish the details along with a call for anyone who recognised the items to come forward. Sergeant Richards was also tasked with making regular contact with the stations in Brecon and Glamorgan in the hope that some information regarding the clothing or the men seen at the colliery might be forthcoming.

The newspapers published on Saturday, February 19, also carried confirmation of a rumour that had been gaining a foothold in the Amman Valley since the funeral of Thomas Thomas. After much discussion amongst its senior directors, the officials at the Star Tea Company had agreed that a reward was to be offered for information leading to the arrest of the killer. The company's South Wales representative, Store Inspector Eardley had contacted the Chief Constable of Carmarthenshire the previous afternoon to inform him that the Star Tea Company was "willing to and desirous of offering" a suitable reward. Following the conversation, the firm announced it would offer "the sum of £100 as a reward to any person who would give such information as would lead to the arrest and conviction of the murderer". The figure was £12 less than the killer had stolen. As part of his duties in overseeing the investigation, Nicholls was instructed to ensure that the details of the reward were published as widely as possible and he personally telephoned the offices of the various newspapers he had come into contact with during the course of the case. The result was the publication of the reward in all newspapers over the following week, with the daily titles publicising the details in their Saturday editions.

While the trip to Ystradgynlais appeared to Nicholls to have been a waste of time, the events which followed the return of Canning to Garnant were to see the Scotland Yard detectives retracing old ground. With the clothing all but dismissed as a clue and nothing new to take the case forward, there appeared little alternative but to go back and re-examine what information they had. Nicholls however remained annoyed by the failure of the Brecon Constabulary to inform him of the discovery of the clothes for three full days and he wondered whether such delays might also occur should any other clue be found. Had the clothes been those worn by the killer that delay could have proved crucial and Nicholls was dumbfounded as to why, with a killer on the loose, he had not been informed immediately. He found himself growing increasingly frustrated with what he saw as the indifferent attitude of the locals towards him and his investigation. His frustration would only grow as the afternoon progressed.

The Deputy Chief Constable of Carmarthenshire arrived in Garnant late in the afternoon to be appraised of the progress made on the investigation and to be updated with regard to the fire at Mr Lewis' drapers shop. Despite public opinion, Nicholls felt the blaze was unlikely to have been related to the murder but remained unwilling to rule it out altogether. While Nicholls and Canning discussed the case as they saw it and laid out the progress or lack of it thus far for the deputy Chief Constable Evans, PC Thomas informed them that they had a visitor.

John Thomas, the brother of the dead man, had returned to Garnant from Swansea to collect from Glanyrafon Villas whatever items of his brother's still remained there. He took the opportunity of the visit to call on the police to find out whether they had anything to report, and to inform them of the conversation that had taken place in the Farmers Arms in Llangendeirne following the funeral two days earlier. Nicholls was astounded. While in private discussions with Canning, Richards and both the Chief and Deputy Chief Constables he had expressed his growing doubt the Thomas Mountstephens was the killer, yet he simply could not imagine under what circumstances the sibling of a murdered man might fail to inform the investigating officer that a key suspect in the crime had been specifically named by a mysterious stranger until two days after the event.

The dead man's brother dismissed the detective's incredulity by claiming he had thought the accusation nothing more than an empty rumour. He had met Mountstephens a number of times times during the period his brother had lodged at Glanyrafon Villas and harboured no suspicion about him whatsoever. It was Mountstephens who had driven to Swansea to inform him of his brother's death and it was with Mountstephens and his family that he had spent that very morning. In the time he had known Mountstephens, he had been given no cause to give credence to the claim that the man was of bad character, let alone capable of murder. Nicholls struggled to contain his anger. It seemed that the dead man's brother was now deciding which lines of enquiry the police should pursue. The manner of the accusation, as it was reported by John Thomas, seemed deeply suspicious to Nicholls. Clearly, the accuser was someone from the valley. None of those who attended the funeral from outside Garnant had any clue as to who Thomas Mountstephens was, let alone that he was under suspicion. If then, the informant at the Farmers Arms was from Garnant why had he waited until the funeral to identify Mountstephens? If he was simply passing on the strongly-held belief in the village that Mountstephens was the culprit, why had he appeared from nowhere and disappeared with equal haste unless he had not wanted to be identified? He would surely have assumed that John Thomas would have passed on the information to the police more quickly than had actually been the case. It seemed possible to Nicholls that the man was simply giving voice to the thought on everyone else's lips, but it also seemed plausible that the informant knew far more about the murder than he was telling. It seemed feasible to Nicholls that the informant had in fact been the killer himself, attempting to ensure the police went off in a different direction.

John Thomas gave his description of the man who had approached him as best he could, but his recollection was almost useless. All he could offer by way of information was that man stood roughly to a height of five-foot-four or five, though possibly a little shorter. He had a thin moustache and wore a hat low over his face. Nicholls could not imagine how or why Thomas had been so dismissive of the man and so incapable of recalling anything but the vaguest of details. The unexpected twists and turns of Saturday were set to continue after the departure of the stationmaster.

Shortly after John Thomas had left Garnant, another visitor arrived at the police station and asked to speak with the detectives. Trevor Morgan, the 13-year-old part-time errand boy at Star Stores, was shown in to the back room of the station where Nicholls, Canning and the Deputy Chief Constable sat waiting. The schoolboy had been interviewed by Sergeant Richards immediately in the days after the murder, and again by Nicholls and Canning following their arrival in Garnant. However, with a week now passed since the crime, the boy claimed that he had only that morning remembered seeing someone lurking in Coronation Arcade on the evening of the murder. When the boy described the man he saw waiting at the bottom of the Arcade to the rear of the Star neither Sergeant Richards nor Nicholls were in any doubt as to the identity of the shadowy figure.

Trevor told the officers that he had returned to the shop after completing his final deliveries of the day at around 7pm and, as he passed, saw the man down towards the bottom of the Arcade, close to the back of Star Stores. Trevor recognised him as a regular customer at the shop. It was Tom Morgan, the one-handed man. "He stated that he was positive that it was Morgan, although he had his back to him, and was some distance from him," noted Nicholls.

The boy claimed he was sure of the man's identity because he had clearly seen him in the light cast from a fish shop in the

Arcade. With his story told, Trevor Morgan departed the police station and left Nicholls and his colleagues in a state of confusion. The errand boy, like everyone else in the village, would have been all too aware that a great deal of suspicion had already fallen on the shoulders of Tom Morgan, not least because news of his interview at the station and Sergeant Canning's visit to Old Anchor House, had – like every other movement and action of the Scotland Yard detectives – spread through the Amman Valley like wildfire. "It is strange that the boy did not mention the fact that he saw Tom Morgan down the Arcade in the evening until a week after the murder for Morgan was under general suspicion in the village," Nicholls pointed out in his report.

Nicholls was, once again, astounded. In London, he would assume anyone failing to come forward with information which might prove crucial to solving the most heinous of crimes did so only with a reason, whether fear, guilt or loyalty to the killer. Within the space of forty-eight hours in this God-fearing West Wales village, three people had come forward with information anyone would surely recognise as essential to the police. However, none could have seriously been considered to have had any involvement in the crime. The sergeant at the Ystradgynlais police station, the dead man's brother and now the teenage errand boy had withheld information that might – had it been made available to the police at the earliest opportunity – allowed Nicholls to make progress. In an investigation which continued to stutter and stall without ever making any real headway in one set direction, it seemed that everyone and everything was attempting to distract the chase for the killer.

Nicholls was forced to consider Trevor Morgan's information and the reasons behind the delay in it being brought to his attention. It was of course possible that despite the interviews and the local suspicion of the one-handed man, the boy had simply forgotten he had seen him in the Arcade until some external source had jogged his memory. It was however also possible that, having known that Tom Morgan was under suspicion, the boy had come forward in the hope that he might be in line for a share of the reward should Morgan be arrested. The delay – and now the reward – meant Nicholls was forced to remain dubious of the sighting and he was unwilling to give it any great value at that stage. However, Trevor Morgan's visit did see the spotlight of the investigation focus on Tom Morgan once again. Nicholls decided that he and Canning would spend what remained of Saturday – it was now dark and well into the evening – retracing the suspect's alibi.

Morgan had claimed that he had called into Coronation Arcade a little after lunch-time on the day of the murder and then returned home for a short time before catching the Ammanford bus to visit his wife at John Wilde's greengrocery shop. Morgan had said that he had then caught the bus back along the valley with the intention of attending Gwaun cae Gurwen Public Hall, but due to the lateness of the hour had got off the bus at the stop close to his home. He had categorically stated that the time had been 7pm or moments after and he had gone directly to his home from the bus stop. After arriving back at Old Anchor House he realised there was no milk in the house and had called on a neighbour, Mrs Williams, to borrow some milk. He had also gone to the chip shop close to Lamb Buildings and purchased a bag of fried potatoes which he took back home to eat. At 8pm or shortly after, he took a slow walk through the village as far as Gellyceidrim Colliery, returning home a little before 9pm or thereabouts – certainly prior to his wife's arrival at a few minutes after the hour. Morgan had been adamant that he had not been to the Star Stores nor Coronation Arcade at any time after his visit in the early afternoon. Nor had he called into any shops or businesses on his evening stroll. His walk, he had said, took him along the valley road only and at no time had he diverted off the main thoroughfare. Following the arrival of his wife in Garnant after her day at work she too had called into the chip shop her husband had visited and bought them each a bag of chips. Ethel Morgan had maintained that her husband was in the house when she arrived back with their supper and neither had left the house at any point afterwards. They had gone to bed together at 11pm or shortly after.

It seemed a relatively straightforward task for Nicholls and his sergeant to confirm the key moments in Morgan's story. However, the individuals whose interactions would go some way to proving once and for all that Morgan could not have been the killer of Thomas Thomas were less concrete than the men from Scotland Yard would have hoped. Canning visited Mrs Williams to ask if she could recall the precise time at which Morgan had called asking for a jug of milk. Her response was a surprise. "She stated that she was almost certain that Morgan had not fetched the milk from her on the Saturday night of the murder," Nicholls recorded.

She told the detective sergeant that it was not an uncommon occurrence for Morgan to come calling with a request to borrow this or that, particularly while Ethel was at work. However, she had been sure that on that particular Saturday, there had been no such visit. Nicholls accompanied Canning and called on Mrs Williams again. However, the presence of the two detectives was clearly too much for the old lady. Initially, she remained sure – or at least almost sure – that Morgan had not visited her on the night in question. However, she became increasing nervous and grew ever more agitated throughout the course of the interview. She began to confuse dates and times. Despite remaining convinced that she had not seen Morgan on Saturday night she could recall handing over a jug of milk one evening, Friday or perhaps even Thursday. It might even have been Sunday. She soon began to doubt herself and question her own memory. By the end of the interview her certainty that she had not handed over milk on Saturday night had disappeared. Nicholls knew that if she were ever brought before a court, her evidence would prove useless.

The two officers then walked the short distance to the chip shop owned by Mr and Mrs Bevan where Morgan claimed he had purchased a bag of chipped potatoes at 7pm and his wife another two shortly after nine. It was after 7pm when the policemen entered the shop and already a large queue of customers had gathered. The shop was a hotbed of activity with sizzling fat, chatter and steam combining to create a bustling, frantic atmosphere. The officers spoke briefly with the couple behind the counter with their conversation interspersed with calls for a fish supper or a bag of chips. Once again, the detectives were surprised by the response to their questions. The Bevans assured the two men that they knew both Tom Morgan and his wife Ethel very well, both were regular customers, living almost directly opposite the shop. They also stated without any doubt that Tom Morgan had indeed been in the shop on the night of the murder. However, according to both husband and wife, he called in and purchased a bag of chips, not some time after 7pm as he had claimed, but between 9pm and 9.30pm, possibly even later. The two policemen found themselves confused. The Bevans were adamant that Tom Morgan had visited the shop at the very time when Ethel Morgan was said to have made her purchase. When asked about Ethel, the Bevans were equally confident that Ethel Morgan had not entered the shop at all on Saturday night, and had certainly not purchased any food.

Nicholls and Canning walked the short distance back to the police station with none of their questions answered – at least not in any way they might have expected – and more added to those they had set out with. The information they had received on their evening stroll made no sense. It seemed utter madness for someone clearly so well versed in the ways of a police investigation as Tom Morgan to fabricate an alibi filled with such specific – and easy to check – detail. It was inconceivable that someone like Morgan would not expect the detectives of Scotland Yard to confirm his story. It was not as if Morgan had been dragged off the street into an interview room and forced to think on his feet, he had had time to thrash out his story – if story it was. The fact his version of events tallied precisely with that of his wife appeared to give further credence to the alibi. All checks so far had shown Ethel Morgan to be an honest and upstanding citizen, a chapel-goer and a trusted shop worker. How could it be that every individual who could prove Tom Morgan's specific alibi correct disputed it?

The men from London sat down with Sergeant Richards once they had returned to the station to discuss the day's events. It was agreed that Trevor Morgan's story should be given little weight. The boy was too young and his memory, only arriving a week after the event, sounded too much like an effort to be a part in the investigation and the potential reward than a definite sighting of the suspect. The very opposite was true of Mrs Williams. Her recollection of the events of February 12 had grown weaker and weaker with the passing seven days and had crumbled before their eyes. That left only the Bevans. Both had been sure that Tom Morgan had visited their premises after 9pm when he claimed he was at home, and both were equally adamant that Ethel Morgan had not been to the shop at all, despite her claim that she had. Unlike the boy Morgan and Mrs Williams, there was no reason to doubt their credibility or the integrity of their claim. They were however recalling a very busy night of trade – their busiest of the week made all the more hectic by the additional people in Garnant who came to watch the Amman Valley derby. There had been numerous unknown faces in the shop and business had been extremely brisk. The only reason then that it might prove possible to dismiss the recollection of the Bevans was that of a natural human failing.

"The Bevans are very busy in their shop on Saturday nights and on that night in particular," noted Nicholls. "There is the possibility that they may be mistaken in what they say." It was however a conclusion which left the detective far from satisfied.

Chapter Twelve:
A good reputation

ON MONDAY, FEBRUARY 21, the Garnant branch of Star Stores at Two Commerce Place re-opened for business under the control of a trusted and experienced manager sent by the Star Tea Company to oversee the return to business – at least on a temporary basis. The day's trading was brisk and the shop far busier than usual for a Monday as the residents of Garnant and Glanaman – and some from Ammanford, Gwaun cae Gurwen, Brynaman and beyond, made macabre pilgrimages to the site of the killing to see what remained of the bloodstains on the floor. From immediately after opening its doors, the shop was filled with whispers and pointing fingers as the people of the valley sought to piece together the information already in the public domain to replay the events of February 12 in their imaginations.

And while the shop – and with it, the valley – returned to some degree of normality, and the people of Cwmaman retraced the well-beaten path to the Star in search of some ghoulish titillation, Nicholls and Canning were also going over old ground. The two men, with Sergeant Richards, PC Thomas and Deputy Chief Constable Evans, re-examined the evidence they had before them, they read and re-read the statements they had gathered in the hope that the new day might bring with it some new insight or a chink of light to their otherwise darkening understanding of the crime. It was agreed that though his actions on the night in question appeared suspicious, there was little reason to consider Morgan Jeffreys a serious suspect. His failing health and age made him an unlikely candidate for burglary, and even more so a man willing to risk a confrontation, even with someone as frail as Thomas Thomas. The village rumour that Phoebe Jones had played some part in the crime by surmising that she had a secret lover who she helped gain entry to the store before she left – either to commit a robbery or to kill or maim Thomas Thomas in a bid to see her promoted to the role of manager, were considered equally absurd. As things stood, the officers investigating the case were left with two potential suspects but no evidence whatsoever.

The case against Thomas Mountstephens centred solely on the fact that he had failed to go to the store when Thomas Thomas did not come home. That failure, coupled with a general feeling in the village that Mountstephens – for whatever reason – remained distant from the community appeared enough to condemn him in the eyes of many. However, both Mountstephens and his wife claimed that Thomas Thomas had warned them earlier in the evening that he intended to work on late into the night. That in itself was not an unusual course for the shopkeeper though it did seem strange that Mountstephens had not grown concerned when his lodger had failed to return by 1am. However, even Phoebe Jones, though surprised her employer appeared to be working quite as late when she returned home from the dance, was not overly concerned.

Mountstephens was without doubt a close friend of the shopkeeper – or at least as close a friend as was possible between two men set aside from the rest of the valley's inhabitants. John Thomas, the dead man's brother, also considered Mountstephens a friend, so much so that when told he was the killer he thought so little of the accusation that he failed to bring it to the attention of the police. While the evidence against Mountstephens was non-existent, the ill-feeling towards him in the village continued to fester. It was also not enough to eliminate him from the inquiry simply because he was the subject of innuendo and speculation.

Thomas Conway Hewitt Morgan was in a completely different situation. Morgan was a known criminal who had spent time behind bars. He was suspected of numerous petty crimes in the area, though none had been proved. He was clearly an intelligent, devious man who had little or no respect for the law, for others or their property. His willingness to provide an alibi detailing his exact movements on the evening of the crime appeared on the one hand to eliminate him, yet had been torn to shreds by the fact that all those he had used to prove his whereabouts refuted his claims. However, it seemed absurd that he would fabricate such a story with so many independent witnesses if it were not true. Morgan was also the subject of rumour and gossip in the village. His reputation was always likely to ensure he would be marked out as a potential suspect for any reported crime from the first. However, his criminal past and questionable alibi offered nothing concrete either in the way of clues or evidence. The key factor in relation to Morgan as a possible suspect was however something even Inspector Nicholls could not ignore. The officers sitting around the table at Garnant police station were fully aware that Dr Jones would state on oath at the inquest that the perpetrator of the Star Stores murder was without doubt right-handed. Sergeant Richards, Nicholls and the Deputy Chief Constable had all spoken directly to the doctor and his firm conviction in his analysis had only seemed to grow during the past week. The doctor's assessment alone was enough to ensure that Morgan was not the killer. His injury made it utterly impossible for him to have killed Thomas Thomas.

Nicholls, though, remained unsatisfied with the doctor's assessment, but he knew that once the physician gave evidence at the inquest – which had by now been moved from March 1 to March 8 due to the lack of progress made during the investigation – it would be all but impossible to consider Morgan a suspect. Indeed, unless the doctor was willing to change his view regarding the right-handed man – or at least confess he was less sure of the evidence than he appeared to be, Morgan was safe. Without Tom Morgan as a suspect, there remained only two possibilities, one of which none of the officers present dared dwell on. Either Thomas Mountstephens was the killer or a person so far completely outside the current investigation was guilty of murder and was still at large, mingling freely, above suspicion, amongst the shoppers, miners and tin workers on that cold Monday morning. With little else to go on, Nicholls declared that he would return to London with the cash box from the shop on which he and Canning had discovered the finger-prints along with those taken from the dead man to have them analysed by the expert staff at New Scotland Yard. He would also take the opportunity of a return to the capital to look into the past of Thomas Hooper Mountstephens and discover whether there was any truth in the rumour that he was of bad character and had been forced to leave London under a cloud. The latest claims circulating in the village said he had run away from the capital following accusations of theft from a former employer.

Nicholls left Garnant by the last train on Tuesday, February 22, making connections at Llanelli, Swansea and Cardiff before arriving back in the great metropolis mid-morning on the Wednesday. Shortly after lunch the Inspector sat down with his superiors, Superintendent Thomas and Superintendent Collins, to appraise them of his situation and admit that little or no progress had been made with the West Wales investigation. After briefing the senior officers, Nicholls took the cash tin for the fingerprints to be compared with the records at Scotland Yard. He was particularly keen to ascertain whether the prints could be linked either to Tom Morgan or, though he thought it even less likely, the missing convict David Lewis. The fingerprint marks were photographed and the images were taken for development. Nicholls also handed over the prints he and Canning had created from the fingertips of the dead man at Glanyrafon Villas shortly after their arrival in Garnant.

While the images were being developed, Nicholls set out for Highgate to discover something of Thomas Mountstephen's past. At 194 Archway Road, he visited the shop of William Gorton, an oil and colour merchant. Mountstephens had claimed that he had worked for Gorton from the time he left school until shortly before he departed for Wales. Nicholls was growing increasingly desperate for a breakthrough in the case and was delighted to find the proprietor on the premises when he arrived. Gorton confirmed he knew Mountstephens and he had indeed spent some eight years in his employment. Much to his disappointment, though coming as no great surprise, Gorton said that there was no truth whatsoever in the claim that Mountstephens had been fired or had been suspected of theft. In fact, Gorton said, Mountstephens had left his employment of his own accord and Gorton had been extremely sorry to see him leave, describing him as an excellent worker and a valued member of staff. "Gorton recalled him as an extremely pleasant young man who bore an excellent character," Nicholls noted.

The detective then visited Ainsley Brothers Butchers of Cranley Parade in Muswell Hill. Mountstephens was said to have worked at the shop for a short period following his departure from Gorton's and prior to his leaving for Wales. Despite the fact he had worked in the butchery for only a matter of months, Nicholls was able to find one employee who had a clear recollection of Mountstephens. "It is said by a man with whom he worked at that place that he bore a good reputation."

Again, there was no truth to the claim that Mountstephens had been fired, nor that he had been in any way suspected of any wrongdoing during his period of employment. Satisfied that the accusations levelled at Mountstephens in the Farmers Arms held no substance, at least none that could be found in his past life in London, George Nicholls went home to spend the evening with his beloved wife Alice and their children Bernard and Dulcie. It was the first time he had seen them in more than a week. With any lingering doubts regarding Mountstephens now all but eliminated, Nicholls returned to Scotland Yard on the morning of Thursday, February 24, in the hope that the fingerprint tests might offer some hope for the investigation. He was again to be left disappointed.

The examination and comparison of the finger prints were carried out by Superintendent Collins. Collins was of the opinion that the prints on the box were of poor quality and were smudged and unclear. He was however as sure as he was able to be that they were completely dissimilar to those held in the files as belonging to either the missing convict David Lewis or, more importantly, Thomas Conway Hewitt Morgan. Collins, in his expert opinion, concluded that all the prints on the cash box were consistent with those taken from the dead man, Thomas Thomas. Dejected and having learnt nothing that might take the investigation forward Nicholls caught the afternoon train back to Garnant.

He met the Chief Constable of Carmarthenshire and his deputy on the morning of Friday, February 25, to inform them that his trip to London had been of little value. Apart from removing the fingerprints on the cash tin as possible evidence in identifying the killer, nothing productive or substantial had been gained. He also informed them of his meetings with Mr Gorton and the staff at Ainsley Brothers which, while not conclusive, only served to undermine the suspicion cast on Thomas Mountstephens of his perceived "bad character and allegations of theft from a former employer". The newspaper appeals for witnesses to the crime and for information regarding the blood-stained clothing or men seen at the colliery in Cwmtwrch on the weekend of the murder had also failed to garner any response. Similarly, the publication of the £100 reward offered by the Star Tea Company for information leading to the arrest of the killer had resulted in nothing.

Despite the decision to delay the inquest, possible avenues of investigation were rapidly drying up for the celebrated detective, who was aware that his reputation was looking more and more likely to be tarnished by his time in Wales. Nicholls however was famed for his tenacity and remained unwilling to give up the chase. Despite the assessment of the doctor, the detective refused to eliminate Tom Morgan altogether from the inquiry. After the meeting with the senior officers of the Carmarthenshire Constabulary, he and Canning went to Ammanford to interview fruiterer and greengrocer John Wilde. The shopkeeper was able to confirm that Morgan had visited the shop briefly during the early evening of February 12 and spoken there with his wife. Mr Wilde could offer no insight into the nature or tone of conversation which had taken place between the couple, but suggested it might have been in relation to Morgan seeking money from Ethel. While he had not overheard any such talk on the night in question, Mr Wilde was aware that Morgan's visits were predominantly for the purpose of cajoling a few shillings from his employee's purse. The shopkeeper made it clear, albeit in indirect terms, that he found Morgan to be a lazy, untrustworthy individual who he felt exploited his wife's good nature and hard work to enjoy a life of leisure. It was Mr Wilde's view that the injury to Morgan's hand had done little to change his attitude to life. Morgan, the shopkeeper believed, had exploited his wife prior to the injury just as he had continued to following it.

Both Mr Wilde and his wife Angharad were however fulsome in their praise of Ethel Morgan and were, to some degree, rather protective of her. She had been employed by the couple as an assistant for more than ten years, prior in fact to her meeting with the man who was to become her husband. They were able to recall the early days of their employee's courtship with the young soldier. Both said they had had their concerns during the early days of the relationship, fearing that Ethel, who was considerably older than her charming suitor, was being manipulated and her loneliness exploited. The shopkeepers assured Nicholls that at no time during her decade-long employment had they ever had any reason to doubt Ethel Morgan's honesty, integrity or trustworthiness. Ultimately, it seemed to Nicholls, the confusion surrounding Morgan's alibi for the evening of February 12 would mean little. Whether he was seen by Mrs Williams, Trevor Morgan or the Bevans prior to his wife coming home was irrelevant. At the time the murder took place, Tom Morgan was in the company of his wife Ethel, a hard-working, trusted, chapel-going pillar of the community. The character reference supplied by Mr and Mr Wilde, her employers of ten years who considered her like a daughter, meant her word was beyond reproach. "They both state that they have never had any reason to doubt her," wrote Nicholls in his report. "It is their opinion that any statement made by her can be relied upon."

Chapter Thirteen:
Nothing in the nature of a clue

WITH BOTH OF HIS MAIN SUSPECTS linked to the killing of Thomas Thomas by nothing more than rumour, Detective Inspector George Nicholls, the man who caught the man who broke the bank at Monte Carlo and apprehended war-time spies and notorious villans, was ready to admit defeat. On the Saturday morning he contacted the Chief Constable's office in Llandeilo and arranged a meeting for the morning of Monday, February 28. His arrival at the Civic Hall in the smart little market town with its winding, medieval streets and stunning bridge over the River Towy, was greeted with gloom. Nicholls sat down once again with Chief Constable Picton Phillipps and Deputy Chief Constable Evans and went through the details of the entire investigation from his arrival in Garnant to his interview with Mr and Mrs Wilde.

"Practically everything that is possible in the case has been done," Nicholls told them.

The Chief Constable accepted Nicholls' assessment. "There was nothing whatever in the nature of a clue," he told the man from Scotland Yard.

Following his interview with the Chief Constable, Nicholls visited Mr Nicholas the Coroner and handed over all the relevant documents, statements and interview transcripts that had been amassed during the investigation. He also presented a list of witnesses that should be called for the inquest. During the course of their conversation and Nicholls' explanation of the details of the case as he saw it, the Coroner expressed a strong desire that the Scotland Yard man be present at the inquest. Nicholls agreed that, with the permission of his superiors in London, he would return to Garnant in time to be present at the hearing seven days later on March 8.

With their train tickets booked for the following day, Nicholls and Canning had the remainder of the afternoon and evening to mull over the case. Despite handing over the files and informing the Chief Constable that no further progress could be made, they chose to have one last throw of the dice. Tom Morgan arrived at the police station late in the afternoon. The news that the London detectives were about to leave Garnant with the case unsolved was already spreading through the Amman Valley. Nicholls was clutching at straws and Morgan knew it.

The detective asked Morgan to run through his entire alibi once again, and Morgan did so – giving an identical version of events as he had offered previously. When Nicholls sought to press Morgan with the inconsistencies in his story and the contradictions put forward by Trevor Morgan, Mrs Williams and Mr and Mrs Bevan, the man sitting opposite him remained completely unperturbed. He dismissed all three as mistaken. Nicholls turned the conversation to Morgan's visit to his wife's place of work on the afternoon of February 12 and Morgan was happy to oblige. He described his wife's close bond with her employees and said that he too enjoyed an excellent relationship with the couple, with both Mr and Mrs Wilde having attended his wedding. He said he too considered the couple more than just his wife's employers and thought of Mr Wilde in particular as a close friend. In fact, Morgan explained, he and John Wilde were in the early stages of agreeing a business partnership. Morgan had been contemplating buying a horse and cart with which he intended to set up a mobile fishmonger and greengrocery business. Mr Wilde, Morgan said, had agreed to help fund the purchase of the horse, the cart and the stock. The full details of the arrangement had yet to be finalised, but John Wilde had promised his full support to the endeavour and the two men had planned to iron out the specifics over the coming weeks so that Morgan could begin work on a full-time basis in the spring. Morgan left the station with a smile and bade Nicholls a safe trip back to London. The detective meanwhile wondered why John Wilde had made no mention of the upcoming business partnership, not to mention why he had agreed to fund a venture with a man he clearly neither trusted nor liked.

On the morning of March 2, 1921, Detective Inspector George Nicholls and Detective Sergeant Charles Canning boarded the passenger train at Garnant Station and made their way to Swansea for their connection. They arrived in London later that day.

Chapter Fourteen:
A very determined blow

THOUGH THE CASE ITSELF remained open, the investigation – as far as the Carmarthenshire Constabulary and the Criminal Investigations Department at New Scotland Yard were concerned – was as good as over.

"There was nothing whatever in the nature of a clue," Chief Constable Picton Phillipps had concluded and no progress, nor any great effort towards making progress, had occurred during the week after the detective's return to London.

Nicholls, in line with the request from the Carmarthenshire Coroner, had sought and gained the begrudging permission of his superiors to return to Garnant ahead of the reconvened inquest on Tuesday, March 8. The man from Scotland Yard had again been forced to endure the long, arduous journey from London via Cardiff, Swansea and Llanelli, to Garnant, arriving late the previous evening. His workload in London had not decreased and from his commanding officers' point of view the time taken in travel and to attend the inquest itself would have been better spent solving new crimes elsewhere.

The inquest was to re-open at 10am at the New Bethel Vestry in Glanaman, the only building in the area which afforded the necessary room for the Coroner, his assistants, the jury, the long list of witnesses, members of the press and what was expected to be a sizeable public attendance. Long before the appointed hour, a large queue had gathered outside the chapel and it was clear that as at the initial hearing many would be unable to take a place inside.

At 10am prompt, the Coroner of Carmarthenshire John Nicholas took his seat, followed by Deputy Chief Constable John Evans. Nicholls had already taken up the place allocated to him in the vestry from where he was expected to consider the evidence given by each witness and make himself available to

143

answer any questions that might arise should the Coroner see fit. The jury, with Glanaman postmaster John Phillips as its foreman, again took their seats almost facing the Coroner. Mr Nicholas began by restating the evidence which had been presented at the previous hearing on Tuesday, February 15, when John Thomas, stationmaster of Mumbles Road, Swansea, had confirmed that the deceased was his brother Thomas, a man of fragile health, deafness and of late suffering from regular headaches, amongst a litany of other ailments.

Before the hearing was able to make further progress, John Phillips informed the Coroner that it was the wish of the jury to again visit the scene of the crime to refresh their memories as to the layout of the store. Following a brief discussion between the Coroner, the Deputy Chief Constable and Nicholls it was agreed that allowing the jury to inspect the scene would assist in their understanding of the events of February 12 and so the three men led the jury on the quarter-mile walk to the store. Their journey was followed by those who had been unable to gain entry to the chapel. As the crowd made its way behind the entourage it swelled at every step along the valley road. Although the store had reopened the week after the murder, the decision was taken to close on the day of the inquest, not least because the entire workforce, the temporary manager apart, had been summoned as witnesses to give evidence at the hearing. Following a lengthy examination of the premises in which Nicholls and the Deputy Chief Constable explained in detail the position and location of the body, the ledger books, the cash tins and various other items, the entire troupe made its way back to the chapel, followed by the crowd who had pressed their faces up to the window of the Star while the jury was provided with a tour of the premises. The first witness to be called once the hearing was reconvened was William Matthews, photographer, of Ammanford, who deposed that he had been instructed by Detective Inspector Nicholls to photograph the scene of the crime and the body of Thomas Thomas at Glanyrafon Villas before burial. He was presented with the photographs held in the police file and he confirmed them to be those he had taken. The images were then handed around the jury where a shiver of disgust moved from man to man.

Mary Phoebe Jones, as the person who first discovered the body, was next to take the stand. She confirmed her address as Commerce House, Garnant, and her history of employment at the Star Supply Stores and that of the other staff employed at the store. She gave a detailed breakdown of the events, as best she could remember them, of what appeared a busy but in the main uneventful day. On the morning of the tragedy she arrived at the shop a little before 9am and spent the morning serving customers until the shop had closed at 1pm for lunch. The shop, as usual, reopened at 2pm and she remained serving until 6pm when she had again left the premises to go home for supper. The shop was finally closed for the day at 8.30pm as usual. Throughout the day she had served behind both the provision and grocery counters. She did not notice any strangers in the shop that day. All those present had been – as far as she could recall – residents of Garnant and regular Star Store customers. The other assistants had left the shop before her after closing time, and she remained with Mr Thomas making up the shop ledgers and reckoning the cash. She finished work at 9.45pm. Mr Thomas remained in the store and before she had left the building he had asked her to check that the rear cellar door was locked and bolted. She already knew the door to have been closed securely, but she had looked down from the top of the stairs as requested and saw that the bolts were on. She then opened the side door and went outside, slamming it behind her to ensure the bolt caught on the latch. She was the last person to leave the place, with only Mr Thomas remaining behind.

Miss Jones was then questioned by the Coroner and confirmed that the back door would have been left open throughout the day and evening though this was nothing strange. She also confirmed that she generally went through the back door to her lodgings for her meals as it was a short journey of only a minute or so, either by hopping over the low wall, or as she usually did walking to the end of the Star Stores yard and then entering the gate at the bottom of the garden to Commerce House. She added that the cellar door would have been barred and bolted roughly fifteen minutes after closing time though it would have been opened again when Miss Richards, the other assistant, took a message to Mrs Jeffreys regarding her dress.

Phoebe Jones was absolutely positive that the door had been closed immediately Nellie Richards had returned from the errand. The Coroner put it to Miss Jones that it would have been no great difficulty for a stranger to have entered the building shortly before the rear door was locked and then to have concealed himself in the cellar until after the staff had gone home. Miss Jones admitted that as the cellar was not inspected after closing time it was possible that someone might have hidden themselves away without being detected, though she thought it unlikely for a stranger to have known that the cellar was not checked after closing.

She told the jury that the till at the end of the day had contained around £126 and described Mr Thomas' procedure in totalling the takings and placing the money in the two tins before putting them in turn in the safe. She described his habit of calculating the takings and balancing the account books on the provision counter. She said that the shop was illuminated by 16 gas lights, though at closing time Mr Thomas had doused the two in the shop windows. She added that the light from the remaining lamps could be clearly seen shining through the window in the rear cellar door. She also added that it would be not unusual for Mr Thomas to remain behind in the shop attending to the books after she had left, especially on Saturday night, though she did not know how long he would remain there on an average Saturday night. She imagined he would remain until he was satisfied that the books had been balanced correctly.

On her return from the concert at shortly after 11pm, she saw that the lights in the shop were still on. She went to her lodgings with Mr and Mrs Jeffreys, but at 11.35pm went outside and saw that the lights were still burning. She went round to the front of the shop to see whether it might be possible to discover if Mr Thomas was still there. The blinds had been drawn, but she peeped in as best as she was able. She could not see Mr Thomas but saw his white coat and apron hanging on the bannister of the stairs. She believed that the shopkeeper would only have removed his shop coat and apron when he was about to leave, but said it may have been possible that he removed the items before finishing work on the accounts, though this was not his normal habit. She repeated that she did not consider it unusual that the lights were on after hours because Mr Thomas was in the habit of remaining behind after she had left for the evening. She then told the court how she had returned home and told her landlady that there were lights still on in the shop though she raised the possibility that Mr Thomas might have gone home having forgotten to put them out, as had happened once or twice in the past. The jury asked her who was present in the house when she arrived home and Miss Jones said that Mrs Jeffreys told her that her husband had already gone to bed. Only Mrs Jeffreys and her son Thomas were still up. She believed Morgan Jeffreys, her other son, was out. She then went to bed.

Turning to the events of the following day, Miss Jones told the jury that she had been woken at about 9am by Mr Jeffreys who called her and asked whether she proposed going to chapel that morning. She said she would not and thought it rather odd as her landlord had never previously made such an enquiry as he was well aware that she was not in the habit of attending chapel. Some minutes later, Mr Jeffreys had again called her. This time he had said that the back door of the shop was open. Miss Jones then "rushed out of bed and went to the back door of the shop".

Mr Jeffreys followed behind her. As she entered the shop by the cellar door she could see that the lights were fully on. She began to climb the steps from the cellar and saw that the safe was open and the contents were in a state of disorder. When she reached the third step she saw the body of Mr Thomas lying behind the provision counter near the butter block. His face was towards her, and there was a pool of blood near his head. She screamed and turned and ran back down the stairs, pushing her way past Mr Jeffreys, who had been on a step lower than her. She ran out of the shop and went back into the house in a state of some distress.

The foreman of the jury returned to the events of the previous day, asking whether Miss Jones could recall who exactly had been in the shop, but she said she would be unable to name everyone who had come in as the day had been particularly busy. In response to a second question, she confirmed that Mr Thomas regularly let customers make their own way into the cellar to choose an empty box in which they might carry home their provisions. Again the foreman asked whether she might remember which customers had been in the shop on the day of the murder and when Miss Jones said she would not be able to name everyone who called in, she was asked specifically whether Tom Morgan, the man with the injured hand, had been a customer on that day. Miss Jones replied that she was completely sure that Morgan had indeed been in the shop for she knew him well enough. The fact that she did not trust him or feel entirely comfortable in his presence ensured she was aware when he was in the store. She could clearly recall him going down the steps into the cellar, but was unable to state with any certainty the time of day when she had seen him though she believed it was some time in the afternoon. She could not recall him coming back from the cellar and leaving through the shop though that was not unusual in itself as she might have been busy serving another customer or he may have left the shop by the cellar door.

The foreman then asked whether she could recall Thomas Mountstephens and his wife visiting the shop, and again Miss Jones said she could clearly recall that they had come into the shop shortly before closing time and remained there for a short time which, she believed, would have been in the region of ten minutes. While in the Star, she saw that Mr Mountstephens was talking with Mr Thomas. At no point did she speak with either of the couple nor did she serve or assist them in any way. She did not observe or overhear any particular conversation between Mr Mountstephens and Mr Thomas, though she did see the former paying his account for goods which had been delivered. She also confirmed that she was aware that in the past Mr Mountstephens had sometimes assisted Mr Thomas after closing hours and she had, on occasion, been present when this had occurred. The last occasion on which she could recall this happening was on Christmas Eve when Mr Mountstephens had remained inside the store helping Mr Thomas to weigh up stock and generally keep him company after she had left for the night. She assumed Mr Mountstephens had helped out so that Mr Thomas could leave as early as possible because it was Christmas Eve. She said she was not aware of any occasion on which Mr Mountstephens had entered or left the store by the back door during all her time at the shop. When asked by the Coroner whether she thought it odd for the lights to be on at the shop when she returned from the concert she agreed it seemed unusual but not overly so.

"It was odd, but still it was no odds to me, because Mr. Thomas was the manager," she said.

The Coroner responded: "I did not say so, but you agree it was strange."

She repeated that on previous occasions, both during the management of Mr Thomas and his predecessor, the shop had been left for the night with the lights full on. She recalled one specific occasion when Mr Jeffreys had noticed the lamps still burning after midnight and he had crossed the valley to Glanyrafon Villas and called on Mr Thomas to return to the shop to extinguish them. Turning to items to be found in the shop, Miss Jones said that there were seven knives in all kept on the premises, one of which was stored in the safe. After being shown items by the police following the discovery of the body she confirmed that one of the shop knives was missing though she could not be completely certain that the missing knife was the one normally kept in the safe. Producing the boning knife discovered in the brook, the Coroner asked "Is this the knife?" Miss Jones agreed that it was certainly similar to the knife which was missing from the shop though she said that she believed the missing knife had had a red handle.

The Coroner asked: "The handle of this is dark brown. Are you inclined to think it is the same knife?"

"If you can account for the discolouration of the handle, then it is the same," she replied.

The Coroner informed Miss Jones that he had no further questions for her, but the jury might wish to ask more of her. The foreman asked whether she was aware of anyone apart from Mr Mountstephens who had ever remained after hours to help Mr Thomas. "No," replied Miss Jones firmly. Returning to the visit of Mountstephens and his wife on the evening of the murder, Miss Jones was pressed to recall any part of the conversation which had taken place between them and the shopkeeper.

"I did not take particular notice," she said, "but I believe Mr Thomas referred to the window of the front of the shop, which had been broken that morning as the result of an accident on the part of Mr Thomas."

Following a short hushed discussion between the members of the jury, the foreman returned to the subject of the lights being left on. He repeated that Mr Jeffreys had previously gone to fetch Mr Thomas to turn out the lights when he had gone home without extinguishing them.

"That is correct," Miss Jones said.

"He did not tell you he went to his lodgings on this occasion?" asked the foreman.

"No," said Miss Jones. "He was in bed when I got home on Saturday night."

"How did you know?" replied the foreman.

"I asked for him," said Miss Jones. "I asked Mrs Jeffreys but she said he was in bed."

Diana Jane Bowen took to the stand and identified herself as the wife of David Bowen of Northampton Place. She described how she had been walking past the Star Stores with her children at "from quarter to twenty minutes past ten on the Saturday night".

The Coroner pressed her on whether she could be so certain of the time. "Yes, Sir," she replied.

The Coroner nodded and asked her to describe all she could recall of the events as she passed along Commerce Place.

"When coming along the pavement opposite the Star Supply Stores, I heard a horrible scream," she said, "then a thud and running over the stairs inside shop. I thought in my mind it was someone coming up the stairs. The scream was a loud one, and it gradually died down, all was calm afterwards."

The screams startled her, she said, and she thought them to be most strange. "I believed the boy at the shop had had his hand in the bacon slicing machine. I did not look in through the window. I was going on as if to look, but after hearing running over the stairs, I thought everything must be all right."

The Coroner asked: "The only thing that caused you any alarm was the scream?"

"Yes," Diana Bowen said. "Everything was quiet when we left."

"And what of the children?" asked the Coroner. "Was their curiosity not aroused by the scream?"

"They did hear the scream," replied Mrs Bowen, "and my

little girl went to have a look through the window. She said she had seen nothing but tins of condensed milk."

"And what then?" asked the Coroner.

Mrs Bowen said she took her children home, pausing only to tell Mrs Michael and Mrs Walters that "I had had a fright and thought that the boy at the shop had put his hand in the bacon machine".

"I told them that everything was all right now," she added. "Next morning, when l was informed of the murder, I knew it to be the murdered man's scream that I had heard. I told a neighbour about it."

Nellie Helena Richards said that she was seventeen years old and had worked as an assistant at Star Stores for four years. She lived at the County Police Station and was the daughter of Police Sergeant Thomas Richards. She was out on her delivery round throughout the afternoon of Saturday, February 12, and returned at about 5.45, working in the shop until the close of business at 8.15pm. When the shop closed she locked the provision window and drew down the blinds. A short time after – once she had completed her end-of-day chores, she went through the rear door to Mrs Jeffreys' house next door and was gone no more than a few minutes. When she returned she entered the Star through the rear door and then bolted and barred it after her. She believed the time then to be roughly 8.45pm. Until that time the back door had been open in the sense that it was unlocked. It had been pushed closed but any person who might have tried the door would have found it open. When she returned to the shop, Mr Thomas was counting money on the provisions counter. She left the premises immediately after passing on the message from Mrs Jeffreys to Miss Jones that her dress would be ready to wear when she finished work for the night. The time was approximately 8.50pm, and Mr Thomas and Miss Jones were then the only ones remaining behind.

The usher, at the behest of the Coroner showed her the knife found in the brook and Nellie Richards identified it as one of the boning knives used in the shop. The Coroner asked whether she was aware of customers going to the cellar to take a box to carry home their goods.

"Mr Thomas often took people to the cellar when they came

for boxes," she replied. "I have previously remarked on more than one occasion that I thought Mr Thomas was very silly to show strangers the cellar when he did not know who they were."

She was asked if she could recall which customers had visited the shop after she returned from her deliveries, but said there had been too many to remember.

"Did you see Mr Morgan, the man with the injured hand, go down the cellar with Mr Thomas?" asked the Coroner.

"Yes, Sir," Nellie said. "I saw Mr Morgan. He was not the only one. Some people were choosing boxes on Saturday night and left by the back door."

It was Nellie's belief that Thomas Thomas had accompanied Tom Morgan down into the cellar and that the shopkeeper returned alone, meaning Morgan must have left the shop by the rear door. She was questioned with regard the visit of Mr and Mrs Mountstephens and her evidence mirrored that of Phoebe Jones. They had been in the shop and left shortly before closing time, she had not heard their conversation with Mr Thomas. She was aware that Mr Mountstephens sometimes stayed at the shop to help Mr Thomas with the stock and had last done so on Christmas Eve.

The Coroner then turned to the errand Nellie had run for Phoebe Jones.

"Who did you see when you went into Mr Jeffreys' house at about 8.45pm?" he asked.

"Mrs Jeffreys," Nellie replied.

"Mrs Jeffreys said nothing about the rest of her family?"

"No Sir."

"Did you see Mr Jeffreys at all that night?"

"Yes Sir. He was in the shop about 7.45pm. He was buying things, and left soon after."

"You did not see him again that night?"

"No Sir. I saw Mr Jeffreys leave on the night in question about 7.45pm."

Nellie's father, Police Sergeant Thomas Richards was next to take the stand. Richards laid out the events of Sunday morning, starting with the arrival at the police station of Morgan Jeffreys, the son, at 9.25am.

"He told me I must go to the Star shop at once as Mr

Thomas, the manager, was lying behind the provisions counter," said Sergeant Richards. "He said: 'His head must have been bashed in, as he is lying in a pool of blood.'"

Richards, along with PC Thomas, then accompanied Jeffreys back to the shop where they found the rear door ajar. "We ascended the stairs and saw the safe wide open – there were some insurance cards and letters lying about. Mr Thomas was lying on his back, with the head towards the window and feet towards the back of the shop."

Sergeant Richards described his initial examination of the body and detailed the situation in which he found Thomas Thomas' clothing and wounds.

"I found that the upper part of the trousers, lower part of the waistcoat, and a portion of the Cardigan jacket open. The waistcoat, shirt and vest had been drawn up, exposing the abdomen. Immediately underneath the abdomen there were bloodstains and a stab," the policeman told the court. "On the left side of the throat there was a gash and bloodstains, and wounds on the right temple and on the left ear. One of the eyes was discoloured, and there was also a wound on the cheek. There were no cuts in the deceased's clothing, and the wounds must have been inflicted when the deceased's underclothes had been moved. The upper set of artificial teeth was laying three or four inches away, embedded in a piece of bloodstained cheese. The lower set was found near the knee. A bloodstained brush was near the head. The shop itself was in perfect order, and everything seemed to have been undisturbed."

The sergeant then described the discovery of the blood-stained iron bar which was used to secure the door from the inside leaning against the wall. It was the view of the police, he said, that the bar had not been used as a weapon in any way, but that the bloodstains were due to the killer removing it from the door to make his escape. He then detailed the arrangements put in place for the removal of the body and its transport to Glanyrafon Villas and the discovery of £4 and a penny in the clothing of the deceased. "In another coat at the shop was found £11 odd and a bank pass book," he added.

"On the Monday morning it was discovered that a boning knife used in the shop and the broom handle were missing. They could not be found in the shop. I instructed two boys to search for them and they found them in the brook in the adjacent field."

The Coroner nodded at the sergeant's delivery of the facts.

"Since this occurrence, I think you and the Force generally, with the able assistance of Scotland Yard officers, have made every effort to discover new facts in connection with the affair?" he asked.

"Yes," replied Sergeant Richards.

"And you are still pursuing your inquiries?"

"Yes," came the sergeant's instant response.

The Coroner then turned to the jury and asked whether they might have any questions.

Following a brief, hushed discussion, the foreman rose.

"Would it be possible that a one-armed man or young boy could have used the brush," he asked.

"Yes, quite easily," the sergeant replied. "The brush weighs only one pound and three ounces."

After hearing the evidence of Sergeant Richards, the Coroner adjourned the inquest hearing until after lunch when Dr George Jones would give his account of the post – mortem examination and a medical assessment of the fatal injuries. Nicholls, who had sat as a silent observer throughout the morning's hearing knew that the doctor's evidence and opinion would prove critical to the entire investigation. The lunchtime adjournment was met with a cacophony of voices as the public gallery which had remained hushed throughout the proceedings burst into a thunderstorm of opinion. As those who had been seated in the chapel vestry pushed out into the Cwmaman daylight they were met by a crowd many times their number who demanded and cajoled a repetition of all that had been heard that morning from tongues only too willing to impart their knowledge and personal insight. Long before the allotted hour was over, the entire village and beyond had been offered a full version of events from a variety of sources. When those who were able to get inside once more returned to their seats, the New Bethel Chapel again fell silent as Dr George Evan Jones took his place on the stand. Nicholls returned to his seat knowing that the next few minutes would determine whether he might pursue the man he was becoming more and more convinced was a killer.

Under the direction of the Coroner, the doctor stated his credentials, position and experience before recalling how he had been summoned to the Star Stores by William Copestake on the morning of February 12. He had arrived at the shop at 9.45am and his first act had been to declare the shopkeeper dead. It was his initial opinion, based on the situation of the body in regard to the degree of rigor mortis, that Thomas Thomas had been dead for approximately 11 hours. Two days later, Jones conducted the post-mortem examination, assisted by his partner, Dr Rhys. In response to the questions of the Coroner, the doctor said that any of the three wounds inflicted on the victim would have been serious enough to cause the death of Thomas Thomas. The Coroner asked which wound the doctor considered to have ultimaltey proved fatal.

"The immediate cause of death would have been the stab in the neck," the doctor replied. "That was the most serious and therefore, I assume, the last wound to be inflicted."

Sensing the absolute importance of the chronology, the Coroner pressed him further: "You think the sequence would be first of all that the battering with the broom, then a stab in the abdomen, and lastly the stab in the neck."

"Quite so," replied the doctor.

"The three causing death immediately?" asked the Coroner.

"Almost immediately, especially in his condition," Dr Jones stated with confidence.

Nicholls sank in his seat. He knew full well where the line of questioning would lead and that, to all intents and purposes, all possibility of apprehending the murderer was now over.

"Is it possible from the position of the wounds to form any opinion as to whether they were done with the right or left hand?" asked Coroner.

"I think from the confined space in which the body was found that they must have been done by a right-handed man, judging by the direction of the stabs," replied the doctor.

A flurry of whispers rushed around the room as the significance of the doctor's words was comprehended. They were met with the stern glance of John Nicholas, the Coroner.

"It would have been difficult to use the left hand with the force necessary in that confined space?" he asked.

"Quite so," said the doctor.

"Would the stabs call for considerable force?"

"Yes, a good deal of force."

"And a determined blow?" asked the Coroner.

"A very determined blow," said Dr Jones.

With his questioning of the doctor complete – and with it any possible case against Tom Morgan utterly and irretrievably discredited – the Coroner asked whether the jury wished to ask anything further.

The foreman nodded and asked Dr Jones for his theory on the abdominal wounds "since the clothing was upraised".

Dr Jones admitted he was at a loss to explain it. "I regard it as evidence of great brutality," was the only response he could muster.

"Would it be consistent with the wounds having been inflicted by a man well used to the knife?" the foreman asked.

"That would be difficult to say, but he missed the blood vessels in the neck," replied the doctor. "Of course; he might have done it in a hurry."

"Would you say that the perpetrator was conversant or not with anatomy?" asked the foreman, pursuing his line of questioning.

"I do not think he would be conversant, no."

During his short spell on the stand, Dr George Evan Jones had cleared all clouds of suspicion from Nicholls' main suspect – and also cast major doubt on any case against the third man on whom local rumours had been circulating. When the former butcher and current landlord of Commerce Place, Morgan William Jeffreys, took to the stand he was not asked to explain his knowledge of human or animal anatomy. Nor was he questioned with regard his ability with a knife. Instead, he was asked simply to give details of his movements on the evening of the murder.

Jeffreys repeated the earlier evidence of the shop staff in saying that he had paid a short visit to the Star at around 7.45pm. He had remained there only a few minutes, he said, and then spent the rest of the evening at the Raven Hotel, Garnant. He returned home at 10.15pm, walking westward along the valley road before turning down into Coronation Arcade at the side of the Star. Once at the bottom of the Arcade, he had rounded the corner and crossed behind the shop and over the wall before entering his own house by the back door. On his way home he said he had spoken to two neighbours at the top of the Arcade. While at the Raven, he saw Edgar Rees and Tom Rees, the landlord and his son who both lived on the premises, and Mr Daniel John Davies, the cabinet maker. Edgar Rees had also held the post of organist at Christchurch Chapel since 1911.

"I noticed that a light was on in the shop," he said of his return to Commerce Place.

Responding to the Coroner, Jeffreys said that a light at that time was not unusual as Thomas Thomas often worked on after hours. He could not say that he noticed anything odd about the cellar door or that it might be open. When his son Tom had returned from work, they went together to the stables to attend the pony they kept there. "On returning we remarked to each other on the light still being on at the shop. It was between 11pm and 11.30pm. After we had returned to the house, I went to bed."

He described sending his elder son Morgan to the farm for milk the following morning only for him to return shortly after to tell say that the back door of the shop was open.

"When I was later informed that the lights were still on at the front I suspected that there was something wrong," he told the court. "I went to the garden in search of Mr Thomas, but without success."

Jeffreys described how he had gone back into his house and called up to Miss Jones' bedroom.

"I enquired if she was going to chapel, but she replied: 'No.'"

The Coroner asked why he had asked whether she had intended to go to chapel, knowing that she was not a regular worshipper, when the real reason for summoning her was because of the lights and the open door at the Star.

"I did not then tell her bluntly that the back door of the Star was open," Jeffreys told him.

He said he waited for a short time before "sending up" to Miss Jones for a second time at 8.50am. The Coroner returned to Jeffreys actions on the previous evening.

"Did it not strike you as unusual to see the lights at the Star

Shop on the night in question? Did you not take notice of whether the lights were on or not?"

"I always take notice when I see lights in the shops of my tenants," Jeffreys said. "I rap at the door, and if I find there is no one in, I usually take a ladder and look in through the window."

"Have you been to the Star Supply Stores previously owing to lights being there?"

"Yes," replied Jeffreys. "I have, because of a burner going wrong in the upper storey. And I have also previously gone over to Mr Thomas' lodgings."

"I ask you more particularly now: when you saw them in the same way as on this Saturday night, have you gone to Mr Thomas to enquire?" said the Coroner.

"No, I have not," Jeffreys replied.

"Did you go to the back at any time after entering your house?"

"After my son came back from work, he arrived about ten minutes after I did."

"That would bring you back to 10.30pm?"

"Yes."

"Did you go out again to the back?"

"After he, my son, had a bath and had supper, we both went to the stables."

"What time was that? About 11?" said the Coroner.

"Yes, about 11."

"You attended to the horses there?"

"Yes, to bed them for the night."

"What did you observe then?"

"The lights still on, and also a light from the fruit shop next door."

"Even this struck you as nothing unusual?"

"No, it was nothing unusual."

"Did you make any remark to your son?"

"I made a remark, I said: "Thomas is here working late at the Star tonight." That was all I said."

"You didn't think it necessary to go to the back door?"

"No."

"Did you go any nearer to the back door when you got back after going to look after the horse?"

"No, I went straight into the house."

"The lights were still reflecting from the window, but you had no knowledge whether the back door was open or shut?"

"No, Sir."

"What time did you get up the next morning?"

"About 8.30am. My wife was unwell so I called my son Morgan to go and fetch milk from the farm. Morgan went across the wall between the Star and our house. While I was at the tap filling the kettle, Morgan said: 'There is a light at the Star, and the door is open'."

"What time was this?"

"This was at 9 o'clock."

"What did you say then?"

"I said: 'Oh, Mr. Thomas is sure to be there; call out to him.'"

Jeffreys described how his son then went to the rear door and called out the deaf man's name, but received no answer.

"What did you mean by that, when you said Mr Thomas was sure to be there? Did you think he had been there all night?

"I didn't know whether he had been there all night, or had come back early in the morning."

"Remember, you said that you were struck the previous night that he was there unusually late?"

"Yes."

"Did you not connect the two things together – the fact that he was unusually late on Saturday night and there again so early on the Sunday morning?"

"I did not just at that moment."

"What did you say to your son?"

"I said: 'Call to Mr Thomas,' and he called, but had no answer."

Jeffreys said that Morgan then told him he would go to the farm and left to fetch the milk while Jeffreys called on Miss Jones.

"Why did you not tell her immediately that the door of the Star was open and the lights on?" asked the Coroner.

"I did not want to be blunt and tell her the first time there was something wrong," Jeffreys replied.

The Coroner turned the witness over to receive questions from the jury. It was clear that they were far from satisfied with the answers he had so far provided.

"In your evidence, you said you did not want to be blunt and break the news to Miss Jones that there was light in the Star Shop," said John Phillips, the foreman.

"Yes," replied Jeffreys.

"You were evidently very contrary. Can you please tell why you then let her go upstairs before you, as she was only a girl?"

"Put your question to me plainer, Mr Foreman," said Jeffreys, becoming agitated.

"Can you please tell why you let Miss Jones go upstairs before you when you believed something to be wrong, as she was only a girl?" the postmaster repeatedly sternly.

"I thought it advisable that as she was a person responsible on the premises that she should enter the first."

The Coroner spoke up again.

"Would it not have been all the more reason to have informed Miss Jones straightaway that there was something wrong, because she was the person connected with the premises?"

"Yes," replied Jeffreys, "but I thought it was advisable not to say anything to startle a young woman."

"There is no question of startling her – she was the head hand, and a person responsible. She only happened to be lodging with you. Don't you think it would have been better immediately to have told her the night before or next morning straightaway? I merely put it to you that that is the effect of your answer?"

"I could not see it was right for me to enter the premises when I had a responsible person there."

"Yet at the same time, you did not think it right to tell the person who was responsible?"

"I didn't want to excite the person," said Jeffreys.

"You didn't know at the time anything unusual had taken place?"

"No, I didn't."

"How did you think that it would excite a person? Did you suspect anything?"

"I was getting to suspect there was something wrong."

"What caused you to suspect?"

"Because the door was open and I could not get any answer."

"After seeing the door open, instead of calling Miss Jones,

you proceeded to make up the fire?" asked Phillips, across the Coroner.

"I simply put the kettle out of my hand and called Miss Jones."

"Miss Jones, in her evidence, said she screamed."

"She screamed: 'Oh, Mr Thomas'."

"Why did you not go to see whether things were all right when you saw the lights still burning the previous night?"

"I have never interfered with any of the properties unless I thought there was some danger."

In response to one final question from the jury, Jeffreys said that he generally entered his house by the back way, and sometimes clambered over the low wall between the rear of the Star Stores and his house though sometime he went through the door in the wall at the bottom of the garden. When he and his son came from the stable, they went through the door rather than over the wall.

Morgan Powell Jeffreys, the eldest son of the previous witness, was called to the stand. The colliery repairman had worked the early shift and then attended the rugby match before going drinking with friends in Ammanford. He arrived back in Glanaman at 8.45pm and spent the remainder of the evening drinking in the various pubs which kept the thirst of Garnant and Glanaman quenched, leaving the last at around 12.30am. He was not aware of there being any light on at the Star when he arrived home some time shortly before 1am.

"I had had a few drinks," he told the Coroner as reason for his failure to notice any lights. The explanation was perfectly credible. Morgan Jeffreys was well known to like a drink.

Shortly after getting up on the Sunday morning, he was sent by his father to get a jug of milk from the farm. As he left the house he saw that the rear door of the Star Stores was open but did not notice whether the lights were on.

"What did you do then?" asked the Coroner.

"I called my father," replied Jeffreys.

"What did he say?"

"He told me to call Mr Thomas."

"You did not notice that the lights were on?"

"No. I only noticed when I was returning at the front of the shop."

"Did you tell your father the lights were on then?"

"Yes. My father told my mother to call Miss Jones."

"Did you go with your father and Miss Jones to the shop?"

"No. I sat on the wall outside."

"Was it not strange on your part that you should not accompany your father and Miss Jones to the Star Shop, instead of sitting on the wall?"

"It was not my business," Jeffreys replied bluntly.

Morgan's younger brother Thomas came next. He told the court that he had worked from 2pm until 10 o'clock at the colliery. When he reached home at 10.30pm he passed to the rear of the Star shop and noticed that the lights were on.

"Did you say anything to your father about it?" asked the Coroner.

"No."

"Who was in the house?"

"My father and mother," he replied

"In your statement to the police, did you not say that you remarked that night that Thomas was working very late?"

"Yes, now I remember."

The response incurred the Coroner's wrath: "You must try and remember. What did your father say?"

"I don't remember now, Sir."

"You had a conversation?"

"Yes."

"What did you do after you came into the house at 11 o'clock or 11.30? You had been bedding the pony with your father, hadn't you?"

"Yes. I waited up for some time for my brother. He came home at 12.30am the worse for drink, then I locked the door."

Thomas Jeffreys was quite sure his brother did mention that the lights were still on at the Star, but Thomas said he had given no thought as to why the lights were still burning. When pressed however he claimed that after feeding the pony it occurred to him that perhaps Mr Thomas had left the lights on because the front window had been broken.

"I thought perhaps he wanted to convey the impression that someone was still in the shop," said Jeffreys.

"Did you mention this theory with anyone else, your father perhaps?" asked the Coroner.

"No," replied Jeffrey. "I have never mentioned the theory to anybody else before now."

With all witnesses who had been in vicinity of the Star at the time or shortly after the murder was committed having been called, the focus of attention then turned to the man on whom so much suspicion had fallen. When Thomas Hooper Mountstephens took to the stand and confirmed his name and address the vestry of New Bethel Chapel bristled with tension. For many of those watching from the public gallery, this would prove the moment when the killer would finally reveal himself under the pressure of the Coroner's questions and the unrelenting gaze of God. Mountstephens began by outlining his relationship with Thomas Thomas and his knowledge of the dead man's personality.

"Mr Thomas was a man of regular habits," he said, "and very closely attached to his business."

Mountstephens said he had visited the Star with his wife and children shortly after eight o'clock on the evening of the 12th, and remained there for roughly five minutes. He was "perfectly acquainted with the premises", he said, and had previously assisted Mr Thomas in the shop after closing time.

"Yes," he said in response to a question from the Coroner. "I know how and where the notes and silver are placed."

On the night of the murder he and his wife returned home immediately after leaving the shop. He could not recollect passing anybody he knew on his way home nor could he recall seeing anyone who might be able to confirm that the family had gone as he had claimed.

"The night was rather dark," he said by way of explanation to the jury.

He told the court that he then spent the remainder of the evening at home, and that he and his wife sat down to eat supper between 11pm and 11.30pm. Asked whether he was concerned that Mr Thomas had not yet arrived home, Mountstephens shook his head.

"At the time did it not occur to you that Mr Thomas was late?" asked the Coroner.

"Mr Thomas had informed me earlier that he would be late," Mountstephens replied. "Consequently I did not get uneasy about it."

Lily Mountstephens went to bed after her supper and Thomas went outside to the corner of the house to take a breath of evening air and look out over the valley. He could see that the lights were still burning at the Star. Arthur Impey arrived home about midnight.

"I remarked to Mr Impey that I never thought Mr Thomas would be so late, but then left him to his supper and asked that he give Mr Thomas some supper when he came in."

"Did Mr Impey suggest going over to the Star to ensure everything was all right?" asked the Coroner.

"I believe he did suggest that we should have a walk over to the shop, but I told him that we need not do that as Mr Thomas had already said he would be late."

"It was now getting on towards one o'clock?" said the Coroner. "Do you seriously say that it did not strike you as a condition of things that would make it imperative upon you to go over to ascertain the cause?"

"No Sir."

"It certainly occurred to Impey, and yet you did not accept this offer to walk over?"

"I did not dream of anything being wrong."

"The effective way to ascertain if anything was wrong was to go over. You knew his health was not very good, and he was staying up to an hour that was altogether unusual. Don't you think it would have been creditable on your part to have gone over and ascertained?"

"I did not think so, no."

Pressed further by the Coroner, Mountstephens was forced to admit that there had been no other occasion that he was aware of when Mr Thomas had remained in the shop up to one o'clock in the morning.

"And this indeed was a Saturday night, going into Sunday morning. You were obviously aware of Mr Thomas strong religious beliefs and his view of working on the day of rest."

"I put it down to his being busy," said Mountstephens, "or perhaps that he had not realised the time."

Turning to the events of Sunday morning, the Coroner asked whether Mountstephens had enquired into the whereabouts or well-being of Mr Thomas after he got up.

"I did not Sir, no."

"Did you not see that his supper had remained uneaten?"

"I did sir, yes."

"And what did you do with the meal?"

"I fed it to the chickens."

A murmur of disapproval rustled around the vestry and spread to those outside who were being fed morsels of testimony from within.

"Is not this a little callous?" asked the Coroner. "You made no enquiries as to the well-being of your lodger – and your friend – on that morning and you fed his supper to your hens.

"No Sir. I took it that Mr Thomas had returned."

"Was there anything else unusual?"

"I noticed that Mr Thomas' boots were not in their usual place in the kitchen."

"And yet you thought nothing of it?"

"No Sir."

Mountstephens said that the first time he began to grow concerned was when he saw the two young boys arrive at his garden gate.

"It was only then for the first time that the other curious circumstances – Mr Thomas' supper having been left untouched and his boots being missing from their accustomed place – began to assume full significance.

"And what happened then?" asked the Coroner.

"The boys told me that Mr Jeffreys had sent them to fetch me so I went over to the shop."

Changing tack, the Coroner asked whether Mountstephens was aware of anyone else helping Thomas Thomas at the shop after hours, "in the way that you have done"?

"No, Sir. I am not," replied Mountstephens. Then, after a short pause, he said: "Oh, yes, there is the young boy Williams, who came along once or twice. He is a former assistant at the shop, and he came there once or twice to help weigh up stock."

"Did you refer to him in the statement you made to the police?"

"Yes," said Mountstephens.

"No you did not," replied the Coroner sharply. "Though I will remind you that the reference you made was to a young man named Davies. I wish to warn you that you need to be very careful in your recollections."

The rebuke did not go unnoticed in the public gallery and another rustle of conversation rippled around the room. Mountstephens simply nodded and apologised. In response to one final question from the Coroner, Mountstephens' acknowledgement that both he and his wife were natives of London who had moved to Wales to work sent yet another murmur around the room. John Phillips stood and asked when was the last time Mountstephens had been in the cellar of the Star Stores.

"I cannot tell you that," replied Mountstephens. "Very seldom I was in the cellar."

Lily Emily Mountstephens replaced her husband on the stand and was asked to recall the visit she had made with her husband to the Star on the evening of the murder.

"The conversation was between my husband and Mr Thomas," she said. "I heard my husband say something about cheese but I was not aware of anything else."

"What time was that?" asked the Coroner.

"About 7.45pm."

"Did anybody see you on your way home?"

"No one that I knew."

The remainder of her evidence repeated her husband's and she was allowed to stand down after the jury declined to put any further questions to her. The Coroner then informed the jury that he had been through the evidence of the remaining witnesses who had been summoned, but who were yet to take the stand.

"I do not think that what they could say would carry this inquiry any further," he said.

Following a short deliberation, the foreman announced that the jury were dissatisfied with the evidence given by Morgan Walter Jeffreys and wished him to be recalled. They were also keen to hear from William Copestake, William Brooks and the boy Richards who had discovered the knife and broom handle. They also wished to hear from a representative of the company.

William Copestake, of Coronation Arcade in Garnant, said that while he had been out getting coal on Sunday morning he saw Morgan Walter Jeffreys and Morgan Powell Jeffreys standing near the Star Stores.

"They called on me for me to see what was the matter," Copestake told the court.

The three men then entered the premises from the rear and Copestake described how they had climbed the stairs in the cellar to see the body of Thomas Thomas lying behind the provisions counter. Copestake then went to fetch the doctor after being told to do so by the elder Mr Jeffreys. He had not seen or heard anything unusual the previous night and had not left the house, as his wife had only recently been confined. After Copestake finished giving his evidence, Morgan Walter Jeffreys was recalled.

The foreman of the jury said: "After reflection, some of the jurors think perhaps you will be able to mention some of the others who were at the Raven Hotel on that particular Saturday night."

Jeffreys was clearly unhappy to find his word being scrutinised once again.

"No," he replied. "I can't say I can mention any. It was quite sufficient to see who served me, and I didn't shift from the place. I generally stand at the bar until I leave."

"How long were you there?"

"From 8 o'clock to 10 o'clock. I stood at the usual place by the stairs, and didn't shift from there until I left."

"Who walked home with you?"

"As well as I can remember, I came by myself as far as the Arcade."

Albert William Hurdley, the South Wales Inspector for the Star Supply Stores, said he had carried out a careful examination of the books and accounts at the Garnant branch, and there should have been put in the safe the sum of £128 0s 2½d, which represented about two days' takings for the store. He explained that the general procedure for a branch the size of that in Garnant would be for the shop takings to be banked three times a week, Mr Thomas appeared to be in the act of making up his expenditure for the week when he was attacked. The shopkeeper had mistakenly placed only a shilling to one side to cover the cost of hiring a horse and cart during the week ahead rather than the £1 which would have been required to cover the actual cost.

"He would have naturally found out the mistake on going through his accounts," said Mr Hurdley, "and might have had to go to the safe for the cash, for the purpose of again checking it.

"Apart from that small error, his accounts were perfectly straight, and he was a very faithful servant of the company. The checking of the stock in hand should not have taken more than a quarter of an hour. There was no particular stress on this Saturday and the last thing that he would have done was to check his cash book.

"There was no need for him to have stopped more than half an hour after the others had gone and the only delay might have been in relation to his discovery of his error in terms of the money set aside for the horse and cart."

Thomas David Emlyn Richards said he was an errand boy at the shop and had assisted Mr Thomas in weighing up the stock on the Saturday evening.

"Before you left the shop, did you use a broom?" asked the Coroner.

"Yes," said Richards.

"What were you doing with it?"

"Sweeping rubbish into a bucket," replied the boy to the amusement of the public gallery.

"After that, what did you do with it?"

"I put it bottom upwards on the side of the safe."

The Coroner handed the boy the broom handle that had been found in the brook and that was believed to have been used to smash in the head of the dead shopkeeper.

"Is this the handle of the brush you used on Saturday night?" asked the Coroner.

"Yes," said Richards with a degree of certainty.

"How do you know it?"

"Because Mr Thomas had marked it on the top," came the boy's immediate response.

William Charles Brooks took the stand to confirm his name and address. He said that he recalled seeing Morgan Walter Jeffreys in the Arcade at about 10.20pm.

"I saw him turn round at the bottom end of the Arcade and go towards the back of his own house."

At 4.45pm, the Coroner began his summing up of the investigation into the death of Thomas Thomas, shop manager of the Star Supply Stores in Garnant.

"I am sorry we are unable to carry the matter any further," he said, "but I have called all the witnesses – after consultation with the police – that can possibly throw any light upon the case.

"We have endeavoured to consider what evidence should be brought before the jury, and it is a matter of regret that they were unable to carry it further than they had been able to do.

"This is essentially a case in which there has been a very brutal crime committed upon an inoffensive man, the object of which was no doubt robbery, and one would have liked to be in a position to bring forward evidence that would have had the effect of preventing in the future any such crime, and, of bringing to justice the man who had been guilty of an unusually despicable crime.

"It has been quite easy to reconstruct the thing now pretty well from the evidence we have heard and from the views that you the jury have taken of the place.

"You have gained a good deal, except the most important thing, and that is to find the person who is guilty of this crime. It must have been someone conversant with the place. It is quite evidently somebody who knew – if I may call it – the geography of the shop, and pretty well knew the habits of the man.

"There was every facility for him – the back door had been open all day long, and it only required the turning of the latch.

"There must be some in the world," concluded the Coroner, "who care very little what crime they commit, and knowing this man, who was somewhat deaf, not in good health, was busy over his books, and that there was a considerable amount of cash available, must have introduced himself for robbery in the first place, but some time between a quarter and half-past ten something must have occurred.

"The jury will probably come to the conclusion that the wounds were inflicted with malice, but there is not enough evidence to fix upon who did it.

"There are many odd things in the case, and it is always

desirable to get as far as possible the exact history of the movements on that night of some of the witnesses who have been called before this court.

"It was for that reason that I ordered the witnesses out of court at the beginning of the hearing, because, if there was any fabricated story, the jury could better test it.

"This was a most cruel and brutal affair, and indeed an unfortunate thing.

"There are some very odd things in the evidence of the witnesses who saw these lights. The jury has heard their explanation, and they said that there was nothing unusual; but took no steps to enquire.

"These people who said they saw nothing unusual in it should have been put on their enquiry for so extraordinary was the hour."

Turning the attention of his comments to individual witnesses – and leaving little doubt as to his inclination toward them, the Coroner said: "Mr Mountstephens said he had seen the lights on between 12 midnight and one o'clock. Knowing them to be of such a strong calibre, he should have made some satisfactory enquiry.

"I do not attribute it to carelessness on Mr Mountstephens' part, for the answer he gave was that Mr Thomas had intimated that he would be late reaching home.

"However, not seeing Mr Thomas coming home, it would have been better had he sent over or made enquiries. Circumstances had arisen to have caused this.

"I would have been more satisfied, and I feel sure that the jury would also, had Mr Mountstephens made some enquiries.

"Furthermore, the criminal had had a very long start before the crime was discovered and this was down in no small part to those individuals who saw that the lights were on but made no enquiry within the shop.

"However, I do not believe less than that the guilty one will eventually be discovered. This case will not prove an exception to the rule.

"Mrs Bowen in her evidence said that she did not look into the shop when she heard the scream. Had she done so, the probability was that as the result of the alarm which would have been given, the malefactor would have been caught immediately, or at least soon after."

The Coroner than asked whether the jury wished to retire to the room set aside for their deliberations to arrive at a verdict in the case. John Phillips, postmaster of Glanaman, stood and said that no such considerations would be necessary.

"It is the verdict of this jury that the death of Thomas Thomas was as a result of wilful murder by some person or persons unknown."

He went on to state that it was the desire of the jury to express their deepest sympathy with the family of the deceased, who was considered a very popular man and a good citizen.

He then thanked the Coroner "for the very able and lucid manner" in which he had conducted the proceedings.

"I am sure the feeling of regret and sympathy is shared by everyone," said the Coroner before releasing the jury. The inquest was brought to a close.

Chapter Fifteen:
There are no grounds

THE DAY AFTER THE INQUEST had taken place there was little left for Nicholls to do in West Wales. It was clear to him that the case had ground to a halt and was unlikely to ever make further progress without some significant and completely unforeseeable breakthrough. The evidence given at the hearing had cast the spotlight on two men – Thomas Mountstephens and Morgan Walter Jeffreys – but no solid evidence linking either to the crime had been forthcoming. Both men were the subject of suspicion because of what they had not done, rather than anything they had done which might indicate guilt. Nicholls did not believe that either man was guilty of the murder at Star Stores.

The investigation was no further forward in and the only significant element to have come from the hearing was to eliminate Tom Morgan from the list of suspects. Dr Jones had left none present in any doubt that in his professional medical opinion the murder must have been a right-handed man. The order or the injuries and the layout and internal space constraints within the shop would, in the doctor's view, have made it impossible for a left-handed man – or someone such as Morgan whose right-hand was all but useless – to have struck the fatal blows. Jones was a hugely respected general practitioner and the most experienced doctor in the valley. If it was his view that the killer was right-handed it would be extremely difficult to prove otherwise. Tom Morgan was in the clear.

It was a surprise to John Wilde and his wife when Nicholls and Police Sergeant Richards arrived at their Ammanford greengrocers shop on the morning of March 9, the day after the inquest had been closed. The unexpected visit must have come as an even greater surprise to Ethel Morgan who believed that her husband was now beyond suspicion following Dr Jones' appearance on the stand. Nicholls, however, remained deeply unsatisfied with the doctor's assessment. After more than two decades spent chasing down the criminals of London, Great Britain and Europe, he had developed an innate ability to judge a man's character. Having interviewed Morgan on a number of occasions he could not escape the fact that Morgan remained high on his suspect list – no matter what the doctor had stated under oath. "We went to the shop with a view to seeing whether anything could be elicited from them that would help to clear up the case so far as Tom Morgan was concerned," Nicholls noted in his final report.

When Morgan had been interviewed at the station on March 1 he had claimed John Wilde was in the process of funding him in a business venture, selling fruit, vegetables and fish in the valley from a horse and cart. Given the clear dislike exhibited towards Morgan by the Wildes it seemed to Nicholls unlikely that they would have agreed to such an endeavour – even out of loyalty towards their long-standing assistant Ethel. The question of the business partnership had been nagging at Nicholls since Morgan had made the claim, and the Scotland Yard man also wondered why Wilde had not mentioned at their previous meeting. Nicholls and Richards first spoke with Ethel Morgan and she again recited her arrival back in Garnant at a little after nine on the evening of the murder. When Nicholls told her that there were no witnesses who could support her story, Ethel simply shrugged her shoulders and repeated what she had already told him. When Nicholls told her that the Bevans had categorically stated that Ethel had not been to the fish shop on the night of the murder, but that Tom had – and at the time Ethel claimed she was there, she told him that they must have been mistaken. Her demeanour and response were all but identical to that of her husband when Nicholls had put the same question to him a week earlier.

When the detective spoke to the shopkeeper about the proposed partnership with Tom Morgan, the answer came as no less of a surprise. John Wilde agreed that Morgan had told him of his plans to set up business in the valley once he had purchased a horse and cart, but the grocer was dumbstruck to be told that he would be funding the venture – or indeed have any involvement whatsoever. "Mr Wilde informed me that this matter had been discussed by Morgan with him about Christmas last," noted Nicholls. "However, he stated that he had certainly not promised Morgan any financial aid."

Wilde told the two policemen that he would have had no intention whatsoever of providing Morgan with money, but he had told him – as a favour to Ethel – that once Morgan had purchased his horse and cart he would provide him with the contact details of a number of suppliers and wholesalers in Swansea. It was clear to Nicholls that John Wilde was of the view that there was little chance of Morgan ever purchasing either horse or cart.

Upon returning to Garnant, Nicholls noted that the trip to Ammanford had done little to progress the investigation apart from underlining the detective's view that Tom Morgan was either a fantasist or an out-right liar. It was clear that Morgan had no qualms about lying to the police. The only question was whether he believed his own tales or simply thought himself so cunning as to be able to say whatever thought came into his head. It mattered little however, and the interviews with Wilde and Ethel Morgan had offered no tangible evidence that could be used against Tom Morgan. "Although they were closely questioned, their statements did not carry the case any further," he wrote.

The following day, March 10, Nicholls left Garnant for the last time and made his way back to London the way he had come, via Llanelli, Swansea and Cardiff on the Great Western Railway, which had once brought such life and wealth to the Amman Valley, but now carried the detective away with only death on his mind. The final interviews at Wilde's greengrocers were to be Nicholls' last involvement in the investigation into the murder of Thomas Thomas at the Garnant branch of the Star Supply Stores twenty-six days earlier.

With Nicholls no longer on hand to push the enquiry forward, the murder investigation ground to a complete halt. The only addition to the case file came from a most unexpected source. In late April, a letter arrived at New Scotland Yard for the attention of Detective Inspector Nicholls. The single sheet of paper was dated March 28 and sent from Canford, British Columbia in Canada.

Nicholls picked up the letter on his desk and read:

Sir,

Pardon me for writing to you regarding the murder of Mr Thos. Thomas of Garnant, South Wales. I feel I must tell you my opinion of the case as I hate to think that such a murderer should escape the punishment he deserves. I know the district of Garnant well, and to find that boning knife in that brook without knowing anything about it beforehand is a little more than I can believe, and I think if your men will question the lad who found that knife in the brook that you will find that he knows something about the murder itself. Mr Thomas must have recognised his assailant, consequently the murderer made so certain he would not live. I may say that I happened to see the account of this brutal murder in the *Herald of Wales* on February 19, 1921, which arrived here last week. It may be useless of me writing from this distance, yet at the same time it may be of value to find the murderer.

I am, Sir, yours truly,
Thos Bevan

Nicholls read the letter and agreed with Thomas Bevan's conclusion that the dead shopkeeper had almost certainly recognised his assailant. Only someone who feared he could be easily identified would have gone to such lengths to ensure Thomas Thomas would not survive to name him. As for the view that Emlyn Richards, the son of Sergeant Thomas Richards and the boy who found the knife, had played some part in the murder itself, Nicholls gave it absolutely no credence.

On April 28, he wrote his response in a memo to his Superintendent.

"With reference to the attached, I beg to report that the knife was found by Constable Thomas of the Carmarthenshire Constabulary and Emlyn Richards, age 14 years, son of Police Sergeant Thomas Richards, also of the Carmarthenshire Constabulary. PC Thomas and the boy Richards were assisted in their search in the fields in the vicinity of the Star Stores by a boy, John Morris, age 15.

Both the boys, Richards and Morris, were employed at the

Star Stores and worked under the murdered man, but there are no grounds whatsoever for suspecting either boy of the crime.

"I beg to suggest that Mr Bevan's letter be transmitted to the Chief Constable of Carmarthenshire together with a copy of this report."

Despite the repeated pleas of Nicholls, Deputy Chief Constable Evans and the Star Tea Company in the press, Thomas Bevan's letter from British Columbia was the only information ever received by the police directly from a member of public during the course of the entire investigation.

Nicholls' response to the Bevan letter marked the detective's final involvement in the case – and was the last document included in the case files. No further attempts were ever made to discover the identity of the Star Stores murderer.

Following the inquest – and with not a single worthwhile clue to work on – the investigation quickly faded. Without Nicholls on hand to provide momentum, Sergeant Richards found his time again taken up by more mundane tasks. Nicholls and Canning were given new cases within a day of their return to London and for the Carmarthenshire Constabulary, the unsolved murder at the Star became something better forgotten than dwelt on by the senior officers. The only effort made in keeping the file open related not to the quest to find a killer on the loose, but in balancing the books. As with all murders investigated by the detectives of New Scotland Yard, the not inconsiderable expenses incurred by officers when they attended crimes outside London were in part met from the coffers of the local constabulary and the local council, with additional expenses paid from the Metropolitan Police Social Fund. There was therefore a keenness to have crimes solved quickly – or not at all – by the local Chief Constables who were eager to avoid receiving costly invoices from the Metropolitan Police. While they had no option but to pay while an investigation was ongoing, they were desperate not to see senior officers from London returning time and again to pursue inquiries.

The Chief Constable of Carmarthenshire W Picton Phillipps had submitted payment requests to the county's finance committee, the clerk of which was John Nicholas, the Coroner. The early expense to cover costs incurred by Nicholls and

Canning throughout the investigation, were met without murmur, but when the two detectives returned to London on March 2 the drain on the county's accounts were – as far as the committee was concerned – at an end. Nicholls appearance at the inquest on March 8 was to cause an ongoing spat between Carmarthenshire and New Scotland Yard, as was his engagement of the photographer Matthews to take pictures of the dead man's body and the shop interior. As the Coroner had specifically requested that Nicholls attend the inquest, it was the view of Scotland Yard that his travel expenses be met by the local constabulary. The finance committee meanwhile felt that attendance at the inquest was part of the ongoing investigation – as was his visit to Ammanford to interview John Wilde and Ethel Morgan. Those two interviews proved that Nicholls had not returned to Garnant purely at the request of the Coroner and therefore the cost of the Detective Inspector's return train ticket should be paid from the Social Fund. On April 8 – one full month after he had attended the inquest in Garnant, Nicholls was forced to inform his departmental chief that he had still not received repayment of his expenses in attending the inquest, which had been verbally agreed by Mr Nicholas. "I asked the Coroner, Mr Nicholas, whether he could allow any expenses either in respect of the photographs which were prepared in the case, or for my attendance, and he said that he thought he would be able to," Nicholls wrote in a memo to his superintendent.

The detective had submitted a claim for expenses in relation to the case which came to more than a full week's wages in Garnant: £3 3s for the cost of the photographs, a further £2 2s and his travel expenses to the inquest. "He said that he would forward same to me," Nicholls noted. "I have not so far received any sum from the Coroner. I beg to suggest that a copy of this be forwarded to the Chief Constable of Carmarthenshire and that he be asked to have the Coroner seen in the matter and ascertain whether he can see his way clear to pay the amounts."

The letter was duly forwarded to Chief Constable W Picton Phillipps who, in turn, passed it on to the Coroner. Mr Nicholas then took it to the finance department of Carmarthenshire Council for a second time. He sent their response to the Chief Constable on April 19. "I placed the communication in reference to the Garnant murder before our Finance Committee yesterday," he wrote. "They were however of the opinion that the County should not bear the costs referred to, and, I regret to say, declined to allow them. I take it therefore that they must be borne by the Metropolitan Police."

The finance committee placed the unenviable burden of expressing their view on the shoulders of the Chief Constable, who wrote to the Assistant Commissioner of the Metropolitan Police on April 25.

"I have taken this matter up with the Coroner who is also Clerk to the County Council and police Committee," he wrote, "and enclose the reply."

"If as I understand Inspector Nicholls attended the inquest at the request of the Coroner would he not have a claim against the latter for his expenses?"

There was clearly a degree of embarrassment in the Chief Constable's tone. "Inspector Nicholls did very good work and rendered much appreciated service to us, and if there is any question of his being a loser in any way I would rather make it up out of my own pocket."

On April 28, Nicholls was forced to write again to his superiors to explain his attendance at the inquest. "I beg to report that my attendance at the inquest was absolutely necessary in order that I might supply any information to the jury should they have desired it; also that I should be able to follow up any new points which might have been drawn from the witnesses. There was also another reason for my proceeding to Garnant and that was to clear up a few outstanding matters in connection with the enquiry – so that although the Coroner did ask that I should attend the inquest, it cannot be said that I attended expressly at his request, and I was not called as a witness, it may be that I am not entitled to any expenses from the Coroner and they fall upon the Metropolitan Police.

"The Coroner in the course of conversation with me said that he thought he would be able to grant me expenses and in view of that I felt it only right that he should be approached upon the matter."

The following day a further note was added to the Star Stores file indicting that Nicholls expenses had still not been paid nor any agreement reached as to who should pay. It seems that rather than continue the spat, the Metropolitan Police opted instead to give up arguing with the finance committee of Carmarthenshire Council. It was left to SG Partridge, Assistant Secretary to the Police Commissioner at New Scotland Yard, to bring the matter to an end.

His letter, dated May 5, to Chief Constable W Picton Phillipps concluded: "I am asked to convey to you an expression of the Commissioner's thanks for the action taken by you with reference to Inspector Nicholls' expenses in attending the inquest, etc, and to acquaint you that there is no question of the inspector being a loser in any way."

The Commissioner had relented, and Nicholls expenses were paid by the Metropolitan Police Social Fund.

PART FOUR

Chapter Sixteen:
Information Unknown

THE CASE AGAINST Thomas Hooper Mountstephens centred solely on his failure to walk across the valley with Arthur Impey in the early hours of February 13. Twice Impey had asked that Mountstephens accompany him to the Star when Thomas Thomas failed to return home, and twice the request was rejected. Had the two men crossed the River Amman in the night and discovered the body of the shopkeeper there seems little likelihood that either would have been considered a suspect yet Mountstephens refusal to walk to the shop at 1am cast him in a singularly bad light. The fact he had, by his own admission, failed to notice that the shopkeeper's boots were missing from their usual place next to his own when he woke next morning and was unconcerned when he found that his lodger's supper had remained uneaten was also used to paint him in the blackest of lights.

It is clear that feelings against Mountstephens were already running high in the days immediately after the discovery of the murder and when the dead man's brother was approached on the day of the funeral and Mountstephens accused, John Thomas simply shrugged it off as idle gossip. Clearly it was a rumour he had already heard.

The case against Thomas Mountstephens was based on the inevitable bias of hindsight rather than actual evidence. If Mountstephens had gone with Impey and discovered the body of the dead shopkeeper he would have been cleared, however – as he repeatedly told Impey, the police and the inquest – the shopkeeper had specifically told him he would be home late that night. It was not unusual for Thomas Thomas to remain behind after closing time on a Saturday night, but for him to have informed his landlord he planned to stay on at the shop clearly implied he expected to be much later even than usual. It does then seem perfectly understandable that Mountstephens would have remained unconcerned when his lodger failed to appear before he went to bed for the night.

The charge of callousness, of feeding the dead man's supper to the chickens, only arose in light of the events which followed. Had Mountstephens known that Thomas Thomas was laying dead behind the provisions counter of the Star then to feed his supper to the hens might indeed have been seen as cold-hearted though practical. In reality, at the time he gave the birds their breakfast Thomas Mountstephens was wholly unaware of the fate of Thomas Thomas. It is completely feasible that he had assumed the shopkeeper had returned home very late – certainly long after he had gone to bed at 1am. Therefore there was nothing callous in his belief that the lodger was in his bed having an extra few minutes of sleep.

Mountstephens' real problem was that he was an outsider who did little to ingratiate himself with the common people of Garnant. While the village was swelled by the large numbers of people who had moved into the valley over the years, most had remained rooted to the lower rungs of the social ladder. Mountstephens on the other hand had done well for himself. While the vast majority of those who had arrived in search of work were renting beds and spending their earnings in the pub, Mountstephens was different. Unlike the rest of the incomers, Thomas Mountstephens was one of the few who was able to boost his earnings off the backs of others. Rather than being a paying tenant, he was the one taking in the lodgers. Rather than frequent the Raven Hotel or the Prince Albert, he established a chess club and made himself its chairman. He lived, not in the village proper, but at Glanyrafon Villas across the river and beyond the tinplate works where he might look down on the hurrying, scurrying ants below who lived their lives on the valley road, with a sense of disdain – whether real or unjustly perceived by those jealous of his success.

The case against Morgan Walter Jeffreys meanwhile centred on three key areas of the evidence – and the contradictions – given in his initial statement to police and his appearance at the inquest. In the immediate aftermath of the murder, the 58-year-old told both police and the *Amman Valley Chronicle* reporter that he had arrived home from the Raven Hotel some time after 10.30pm and that he and his son Thomas had left Commerce House and gone to bed the ponies for the night between 11.30pm and midnight. This claim was supported by Thomas when he gave an explanation of his own movements. He told Sergeant Richards that he had also arrived home at around 10.30pm. Both men initially stated that it was only after Thomas had bathed and eaten his supper that they had gone together to the stables. However, by the time of the inquest on March 8, Morgan Jeffreys told the court that he had gone to bed between 11pm and 11.30pm on the night of the murder. Thomas Morgan, in his evidence, also told the court that he and his father had arrived back at the house between 11pm and 11.30pm. But, Morgan Jeffreys initially stated that he had not left the house before 11.30pm and had then walked with his son to the stables at least 15 or 20 minutes away, carried out the chores required of them there and then made the journey back. The entire task – including journey time – would almost certainly have taken up to an hour, possibly even more. Had the two men left the house at 11.30pm as Morgan Jeffreys first claimed, he and his son could not feasibly have returned to the house before 12.30am.

The key issue with Morgan Jeffreys' explanation of his movements centres on his claim that Thomas had had a bath and his supper before the two men left Commerce House for the stables. Thomas Morgan had finished his shift at Gellyceidrim Colliery at 10pm and at 10.30pm he arrived outside the Star and noticed that the lights were still on. It would have been impossible for him to get into the house, bathe, eat his supper then go with his father to bed the ponies and be home again by 11pm.

Phoebe Jones maintained throughout her interviews and then her appearance at the inquest that she left the concert at 11pm and was home shortly after. When she arrived at her lodgings, Mrs Jeffreys told her that her husband was already in bed. Thomas Jeffreys was in the house. Phoebe remained indoors for a short while but checked the time before she went outside to peer through the windows of the Star. It was 11.35pm when she left the house. At no time did Phoebe see Morgan Jeffreys on the night of February 12 and even when she expressed concern at the lights still burning at the Star no effort was made to rouse Mr Jeffreys from his bed, despite his having been known to express concern previously when the lights had been left on.

It is conceivable that Morgan Jeffreys simply got his times wrong in the days immediately after the murder. Had he and Thomas left the house at the time he originally claimed, he would surely have been present in the house when Phoebe Jones returned home – his son certainly was. Perhaps Thomas Jeffreys also got his times slightly wrong. Perhaps he had arrived home and noticed that the Star lights were on 10 or 15 minutes earlier than he told police. Perhaps he had bathed quickly, eaten his supper in haste and gone with his father to bed the ponies before 10.30pm – or perhaps the two men had set off to tend the animals immediately after he arrived home from work and he had not bathed and eaten until returning to the house for a second time. Either way it is believable that Phoebe's arrival back from Stepney Hall had been closer to 11.30pm than she imagined. It is possible that the father and son had dealt with the animals and returned to Commerce House, with Morgan Jeffreys retiring immediately to bed, before the lodger got back from the concert. However, the changing times given in the various statements and evidence of Morgan Jeffreys was a cause for disquiet amongst a population desperate to discover the identity of the killer in their midst. The contradictions in Morgan Jeffreys' statements were enough to cast a dark shadow over everything he said – and also the word of members of his family.

The second reason for the spotlight of doubt to fall on Morgan Jeffreys emerged immediately after the story of the murder began to circulate through Garnant. William Brooks was in no doubt whatsoever that he had seen the landlord of Star Stores in the shadows of Coronation Arcade at 10.20pm on the night of the murder. Brooks had come straight from his shift at the tin-plate works and knew precisely how long it would have taken him to get the point outside his mother-in-law's front door where he could look up through the Arcade to the valley road – at least to within a minute or two. Morgan Jeffreys did not ever dispute that he was seen by Brooks in the Arcade. In fact the sighting only served to reinforce his version of the events of February 12. He claimed he had spent the evening at the Raven

Hotel, leaving shortly after 10pm and getting home around 10.15pm or thereabouts. He gave as witnesses the names of the pub landlord and his son and a local cabinetmaker, though none were ever called to confirm they had seen him at the bar. The fact Morgan Jeffreys said he was unable to recall seeing or speaking to anyone else in the pub during the two-and-a-quarter hours he spent there on a busy Saturday night infuriated the inquest jury, but was certainly not enough to see him tried for murder.

Of far more concern to the public in Garnant – and in part to Nicholls and the other police officers, was why Jeffreys had made no attempt to check whether Thomas Thomas was still inside the store when he saw the light on after returning home from the pub. Morgan Jeffreys, by his own admission – and the evidence of others – had on previous occasion gone to fetch Mr Thomas and his predecessor when they had left the lights on in the shop. He told the inquest that he had also, on a previous occasion, got a ladder which he had used to peer in through the windows of his premises to ensure all was well when spotting lights burning late into the night. It was well known throughout the village that Morgan Jeffreys kept a very close watch on his properties and his tenants, yet on the night of February 12 he did not even attempt to see if Thomas Thomas was still inside. He neither tapped on the store-front windows nor tried the rear cellar door. Despite seeing that the lights were burning at a time when he would have expected them to be extinguished and the shop thrown into darkness, he simply ignored the facts immediately before his face and went home.

Perhaps most damning fact of all in the eyes of the general populace of the valley was Morgan Jeffreys' actions on the morning of Sunday, February 13. He knew as well as any of the strict views of Thomas Thomas in relation to working on the Lord's day, yet when his son Morgan informed him that the rear door of the Star was open he did nothing. When Morgan returned a second time and told him that the lights were on he did nothing still, but merely told his son to poke his head around the open door and give Mr Thomas a shout. How he imagined a man deaf in one ear and partially deaf in another might hear such a call he failed to explain. He also failed to explain why it took him so long to rouse Miss Jones and why, when he finally did call her it was to ask whether she planned to attend chapel that day, despite knowing she very rarely attended services. Rather than raise the alarm, he instead made himself a cup of tea and only then, some ten minutes later did he call Miss Jones a second time and inform her that the back door of the Star was open and the lights were on. He told the inquest that he had not wished to alarm the young lady, but then – fearing something had occurred – sent her into the shop in front of him. The inquest jury clearly felt his reasoning was a contradiction. He had, he said, wished to protect Miss Jones from alarm yet then allowed her to enter the shop before him. He had sent her in first because she was a person of responsibility in the shop, yet he had woken her with some absurd question regarding chapel. Either he viewed her as a weak and timid woman who might easily be alarmed or he recognised her as a senior employer of Star Stores with a level of responsibility. He could not claim both.

It certainly seemed to the people of Cwmaman that Morgan Jeffreys had known more about the murder than was being told. He appeared to have gone out of his way on Sunday morning to ensure he was not the one who raised the alarm that the door was open nor be the one to first venture inside. It seemed instead that he had deliberately woken Miss Jones with his enquiry regarding chapel in the hope that she might get out of bed and notice the Star was open herself. That she might climb the cellar steps alone and discover the body without there being any knowledge he was aware that something untoward had occurred.

Morgan Jeffreys was seen lurking in Coronation Arcade close to the rear of Star Stores at the exact moment when Thomas Thomas was murdered. He was there at the time Diana Bowen and her children had heard the awful scream. He was at the rear of the Star Stores at precisely the moment the murderer would have been making his escape, and yet he saw nothing and did nothing. By his own reckoning, Morgan Jeffreys would have passed the rear door of the Star Stores three times between 10.20pm and 11pm. He knew the lights were on, but he did not see that the rear door was open. He did not enquire as to the well-being of the shop manager or raise a fuss that the lights might have been left burning when the shop was left unattended.

He did nothing at all – he claimed he saw no reason to – and his actions the following morning, were merely those of someone trying not to startle his lodger. To the people of the Amman valley, it appeared that Morgan Jeffreys knew far more than he was letting on.

Of the three men considered the main suspects for the murder at Star Stores, Thomas Conway Hewitt Morgan found himself in a very different situation to the two who became the subject of bar room gossip. Both Thomas Mountstephens and Morgan Jeffreys came under the increasing scrutiny police and public as details of their actions on the night of Thomas Thomas' death emerged.

Tom Morgan however, was a suspect from the very first. His criminal past and reputation in the village inevitably saw the finger of suspicion pointing towards him – as it did when almost any crime was committed. However, unlike Mountstephens and Jeffreys, for whom the confusion surrounding the events of February 12 opened up the possibility that one might be the culprit, the accepted consensus of what had occurred behind the blinds of Number Two, Commerce Place, eliminated Morgan from the investigation. While many considered the case against Mountstephens or Jeffreys, circumstances ensured it was the case in favour of Tom Morgan which saw him fade out of the reckoning.

The two key issues in Morgan's favour were the alibi provided by his wife Ethel and, far more importantly, Dr Jones' assessment that the killer had to have been right-handed. That key medical evidence was to prove crucial in ruling Morgan out of the investigation. Nicholls clearly doubted that the doctor, for all his expertise, could be so sure that the narrative he had developed from the injuries was correct.

Dr Jones' reasoning was straightforward enough. He was of the view that each of the three injuries – the battering of Thomas Thomas' head with the broom handle, the deep stab wound to the stomach and the knife wound to the throat – were each, in their own way, serious enough as to have proved fatal. Any of the injuries suffered by the victim "would have caused death" for someone of such weakened health as Thomas Thomas, he told the inquest jury. He assumed, reasonably enough, that the knife wounds would have followed each other and that the use of the broom handle as a club was a separate and distinct element, albeit of the same assault. His conclusion regarding the order of the injuries was based purely on what he considered to be the seriousness of each.

He had told the jury that the neck wound would have been the ultimate cause of death because it was "the most serious" and therefore "the last wound to be inflicted". His entire assessment of the events at Star Stores was constructed on the basis that because he considered the neck wound to be the most serious it must have been the final injury sustained. Given then that it would seem most unlikely that a killer would change weapons midway through an attack only to then revert to his original choice to finish off his victim, it was accepted that the assault with the broom handle must then have been the opening salvo in the attack.

"You think the sequence would be first of all that of the battering with the broom, then a stab in the abdomen, and lastly the stab in the neck," the Coroner had asked. "Quite so," Dr Jones had replied.

And with those two simple words, Dr George Evan Jones ultimately cemented the view that Tom Morgan could not possibly have killed Thomas Thomas.

The time-line of the injuries sustained by the shopkeeper was to prove crucial in exonerating Morgan, or at least removing him from the suspect list – not for any medical reason but simply because the internal lay-out of Star Stores made it so. The dead man was found lying on his back partially behind the provisions counter to the left of the shop when entering from the doorway leading to the cellar. His feet were closest to the door and his head towards the window looking onto the valley road. Thomas Thomas was lying diagonally across the floor between a barrel and a large storage box. His head was in a pool of blood against a wooden margarine box on the bottom shelf directly behind the provisions counter.

Dr Jones' hypothesis, based on his reconstruction of the injuries, was that the killer had most likely been caught red-handed taking the cash tins from the safe when the shopkeeper came from the shop interior towards the storeroom. Dr Jones was of the view that, upon being spotted, the killer had grabbed whatever was closest to hand, namely the sweeping brush, and smashed the shopkeeper in the head with it, using such force as to send the broomhead flying. Further blows would have knocked Thomas Thomas to the floor behind the counter. The doctor's belief was that an attacker coming through the door between the storeroom and the shop to swing a broom at the shopkeeper would have been seriously impeded if the weapon was held in his left-hand. The wall and shelving behind the provisions counter – the far left of the store – would have made it all but impossible for a blow of any real force – and certainly not one which could have caused the head injuries suffered by the dead man. It was the doctor's opinion, he told the inquest jury, that "the confined space" inside the shop ensured the blows struck with the broom "must have been done by a right-handed man".

However, the fact that the majority of the head injuries were focussed on the right side of the shopkeeper's head meant, if the doctor was correct and the broom was the first weapon used, Thomas Thomas had already turned away from his attacker and was actually being struck from behind by a right-handed assailant. The logic of the doctor's comments dictates that having been spotted and recognised by the now prone Thomas Thomas, the killer realised he faced no alternative but to commit murder if he wished to escape detection. Once the shopkeeper had been knocked to the floor, the killer must then have thrown aside the broom and gone back to the safe where he would have spotted the boning knife which both Phoebe Jones and Nellie Richards said was kept there. With the shopkeeper already flat on his back behind the provisions counter, the killer knelt down and undid the top buttons of Thomas Thomas' trousers and pants as well as the lower buttons of his cardigan and waistcoat. The vest, shirt and waistcoat had then been pulled up to expose naked flesh before the stabs to the abdomen. The killer then stabbed Thomas Thomas in the throat, the knife entering from the right-hand side, passing up through the mouth to sever the root of the tongue and left tonsil before almost passing out through the left-hand side of the neck.

As with the blows struck by the broom, the doctor was sure that the stab wounds must have been inflicted by a right-handed man due to the space restrictions behind the provisions counter. When questioned by the Coroner, Dr Jones had said that the confined space coupled with "the direction of the stabs" and the required force made it all but impossible to imagine a left-handed man using the knife behind the counter.

The very fact that the Coroner continued to press the doctor on the possibility that the murder had been committed by a left-handed man leaves no doubt that Tom Morgan was still, until the doctor gave evidence at least, considered high on the list of suspects.

The doctor was neither asked nor offered any opinion as to when the lump of cheese embedded in the dead man's dentures – which were found on the floor close to the body – had been forced into Thomas Thomas' mouth as a makeshift gag. Nor was he asked to offer any explanation as to how or why the lower part of dead man's dentures were found close to his knee and the upper part behind his head. As for his considered view on what the nature of the injuries might say about the attack, Dr Jones replied simply: "I regard it as evidence of great brutality."

In reality, his evidence painted a very different picture. The narrative of the assault, as constructed from Dr Jones' evidence, was one which began with great brutality but became more measured and deliberate with each passing moment. The doctor depicts a killer whose initial response on being discovered is to lash out with the first thing to hand – and in a wild and brutal fashion, only then to retrace his steps and choose a more lethal weapon. A killer who, after battering his victim into semi-consciousness, takes the time to delicately unbutton the shopkeeper's clothing, stab him in the stomach and then fix the garments. With blood presumably gushing from the wounds already caused, the murder then leans over the prone Thomas Thomas and almost face to face slashes open his throat. The actions as described by Dr Jones are not those of a burglar caught in the act, but of a psychotic sociopath, savouring the kill. The reality of his testimony is that the narrative he describes appears to be one created to fit his assumptions rather than based on any of the evidence, including his own.

Even starting from the view that the blow to the head with the broom came first, followed by the stab to the stomach and then finally the throat wound, Dr Jones' conclusion that the killer had to be right-handed appears deeply flawed, unless the killer was chasing Thomas Thomas through the shop and striking him from behind with the broom handle. Ignoring the doctor's basic premise and taking into account only the available facts, however, throws a completely different light on the events at Star Stores – and indeed the possibility that Tom Morgan may have been the killer.

The distribution of blood around the shop during the assault would have told a great deal about the injuries, and Nicholls must have been more furious even than his calm, calculated case report implies that all traces had been removed by the good women of Garnant the day before he arrived in Wales. The view that the killer was caught attempting to take the money from the safe after Thomas Thomas had finished balancing his books and before he had locked the safe appears reasonable. Phoebe Jones stated in interview and on oath that only after her employer had finished settling the shop accounts on the grocery counter would he place the money in the tins, put the smaller into the larger, and then place them in the safe. He would then return to the grocery counter to collect the various account books, till rolls, receipts and other paperwork before returning to the safe for a second time. Once the various documents were placed inside the safe and locked securely away he would at last leave for the night. The fact that the tins were scattered on the floor in the storage room close to the safe while the account books remained on the counter makes it clear that the killer saw his window of opportunity in those few seconds. Presumably he waited in the shadows until the shopkeeper placed the tins in the safe and stepped back towards the shop interior before darting from his hiding place to grab the money tins. It seems a fair assumption to think that Thomas Thomas, despite his partial deafness, heard something to attract his attention and turned back towards the store room and the safe where he confronted his killer kneeling at the open safe.

That the killer had gone into Star Stores unarmed is clear from the fact that the weapons used were both taken from the premises. If he was caught in the act of attempting to take the money tins from the safe he would then most likely, as Dr Jones surmised, have grabbed the first weapon within reach. The weapon that was within reach was not the broom, which was leaning on the wall near the safe. The closest weapon to hand – if the killer was kneeling or crouched at the safe – would have been the boning knife, which was within easy reach and in clear sight. If such a reading of the scene were to be correct then clearly the killer would have been in no position to carefully unbutton the shopkeeper's clothing before stabbing him in the stomach. The far more likely scenario would have seen the killer leaping to his feet and plunging the blade deep into the shopkeeper's throat.

Dr Jones, in his post-mortem examination, described the wounds to the throat as caused by the blade entering "on the right side of the neck" two inches below the lower jaw bone. The track of the wound "was found to pass upwards and inwards just missing the carotid sheath and contents, passing underneath the floor of the mouth, cutting through the root of the tongue, passing through the left tonsil and almost passing out on the left side of the neck". The blade entered from the right side with an upward thrust arcing left. Such a wound is far more consistent with a blow struck by an assailant coming up from below the victim. Dr Jones told the inquest that the blow had been struck "with considerable force" – a degree perhaps far more in keeping with the upward momemtum of a killer springing to his feet and lunging at his victim with the blade than one kneeling over an already dying victim on his back. The fact that the blade entered the right side of Thomas Thomas' throat and moved across the throat in leftwards trajectory leaves no doubt that the blow was struck by a left-handed person facing his victim. The initial examination of Thomas Thomas' body while still at the scene of the crime reported that the dead man's left hand and wrist were covered in blood yet there were no traces "of that vital fluid" on his right hand. This again gives weight to the theory that the wound to the throat came when Thomas Thomas was able to respond automatically. The natural reaction to suffering a sudden, open wound to the right-side of the throat would be to reach up across the body to staunch the flow of blood with the left hand.

Undoubtedly such a blow would have sent the frail shop

manager reeling backwards onto the floor behind the provisions counter. It was, most likely, during this initial attack that the shopkeeper gave out his "awful screech". However, despite Dr Jones' claim that the neck wound would have been "the most serious" and ultimately fatal, it missed the carotid sheath. Furthermore, the doctor's initial assessment that that blade had "severed the carotid artery and the jugular vein" was incorrect. Following the post-mortem he noted that the knife had "missed the major blood vessels in the neck".

Seriously injured and undoubtedly dying, though quite possibly not as quickly as the doctor maintained, Thomas Thomas would have found himself lying on the floor behind the provisions counter in a spreading pool of his own blood. Though death may well have been inevitable under the circumstances, it would not have been immediate and it almost certainly would not have come quietly. There is every chance the dying man was coughing and choking on his own blood which would have been filling his throat from the wound inside his mouth, he may indeed have still be able to speak – perhaps even scream out. Despite having the knife still in his hand, the killer's first thought was most likely one of shutting up his victim rather than finishing the job. He must have grabbed the first thing he could find to halt the moans and ungodly sobs emanating from the prone shopkeeper. The closest thing to hand was a block of cheese on the counter. To shove the cheese into Thomas Thomas' mouth and wedge it between his jaws, the killer must have all but get on top of the dying man.

For any assailant kneeling face to face over his victim with a knife still in his hand, the next blow would almost certainly be a stab to the stomach. The post-mortem report states that the blade entered a little below the sternum, passed through the left lobe of the liver and along the small curvature of the stomach, making an incision into the stomach in passing over it, and then passing through the left kidney. As with the neck would the trajectory of the abdominal wound, starting centrally and moving from right to left implies that the blow would have been struck by a left-handed attacker facing the victim.

Why the killer chose to unbutton the shopkeeper's trousers and waistcoat remains a mystery though there are a number of possibilities, all of which are nothing more than pure speculation and without any evidential support. Perhaps the shopkeeper had planned a trip to the toilet and begun unbuttoning his fly moments before the attack took place and the killer tidy his clothes out of some perverse sense of decency.

It is perfectly feasible that despite his throat being slashed, a block of cheese rammed into his mouth and a deep stab wound to the abdomen, Thomas Thomas would have remained alive throughout the ordeal. The knife used to inflict the wounds meanwhile would have been soaked in blood. By the time it had been withdrawn from the flesh of Thomas Thomas for a second time it would have been as slippery as the proverbial eel, particularly for a man with only one hand – and a hand which was not the one he had spent a lifetime mastering, but one he was still getting used to using having only lost the use of the other some six or so months earlier. There were two superficial scratches close to the point of the stomach wound but neither went much deeper than breaking the skin. These minor wounds might be indicative of someone attempting – and failing – to make further stabs while unable to grip the slippery, blood-soaked handle of a knife – particularly someone not yet completely comfortable using their left hand.

With his primary weapon now useless and his victim still alive, the killer must have been forced to seek another means of permanently silencing Thomas Thomas. Apart from the cans and jars on the shelves behind the provisions counter, the only thing evenly remotely resembling a weapon was the broom leaning up against the wall by the safe just a few feet away and which the killer would have spotted – either while he was kneeling at the safe or as he searched the shop for something to end the shopkeeper's life. He may have seen Emlyn Richards place it there from the darkness of the cellar shadows. With his victim lying on the floor behind the provisions counter, wedged between the barrel and the large storage box, and with his head raised up and turned against the wooden boxes on the shelves, the killer swung the broom – not in a sideways arc as Dr Jones imaged – but downwards. Raising it up above his head and swinging it like a pendulum to impact on the shopkeeper's skull. It is quite likely that that first blow was struck with such force that the impact with Thomas Thomas' temple knocked the broomhead off and sent it skidding along the floor further behind the provisions where it remained until the arrival of the police next day. It may even have been that first blow which rained down with such ferocity that sent the dying man's dentures flying from his mouth. Dr Jones offered no insight into the number of blows to the head Thomas Thomas received, and by his explanation of events – namely that the killer used the broom while the shopkeeper was still standing – it would have been unlikely that the number of strikes to the head could have been many. His port-mortem examination however tells a very different story. Even his initial assessment of the body while still at the scene fails to match his explanation with Thomas Thomas being struck while still standing.

"On the scalp of the dead man on the right side of the head were two incised wounds down to the covering of the bone," he recorded after visiting the scene. "The right side of the face and temple were badly bruised and swollen and the lobe and helix of the right ear were cut. There was also a bruise on the left temple and around the left eye. "There was a fracture on the right side of the skull of the temporal bone and part of the frontal bone. "There was a bruise on the right temple bone, and a big bruise over the left temple, and three cuts on the right ear."

Even from that first viewing it is clear that the majority of the injuries suffered by Thomas Thomas came from blows to the right side of his face. It would have been impossible for a right-handed man to have struck such blows if his victim were standing, unless the shopkeeper had been attempting to run away and was struck sideways with a blow originating from behind him. Even then, one blow might have been possible for a fast-moving attacker, but the preliminary examination clearly noted "two incised wounds down to the covering of the bone" on the right side of the face. Thomas Thomas would have had to stand and wait, still with his back to his attacker, for the second blow to land before falling or making any attempt to move. The post-mortem examination only served to further underline the fact that the majority of the injuries were sustained by the right side of Thomas Thomas' head. Nicholls recorded in his report to Scotland Yard the key injuries discovered by Dr Jones.

"On removing the scalp he found a fracture of the squamous portion of the right temporal bone and parts of the front and right parietal bone which were in contact with the temporal bone.

"There were eleven pieces of bone and they were pressing on the membranous coverings and the brain itself. The zygoma was also fractured in two places."

Eleven pieces of bone were pressed into the membranous coverings of the brain. It is extremely hard to imagine the amount of force required to cause an impact from an item as brittle as a broom handle on a standing man who would stumble and fall, absorbing and redirecting the impetus of the blow which might smash the strongest bone in the human body into so many pieces. Were the victim instead to be lying flat on his back with his head pressed up against a hard wooden box at the time of repeated impacts, then it is more than feasible that even a bone as thick and solid as the human skull would fracture.

The small cuts to Thomas Thomas' head, face and right ear were measured and matched the two nails sticking out from the broom handle discovered in the stream and which had been hammered into to secure the broomhead for use in the shop. The presence of these small cuts also clearly indicates that that the broom was used repeatedly to strike Thomas Thomas in the head after the broomhead had come off. The fact that the box against which Thomas Thomas head was pressed was splattered with blood to a height far greater than the head itself also implies that the injuries were sustained once he was already in that position. It might well be worth returning to the question of which injury is likely to cause the more immediate death, a slash to the throat that misses all major blood vessels, or repeated blows to the head causing eleven pieces of the skull to become embedded in the brain.

The injuries to the head, if suffered while Thomas Thomas was already lying prone behind the provisions counter, also appear to lessen the likelihood of the killer being right-handed. In fact, if the victim was lying on his back behind the provisions counter and the injuries inflicted by the broom came after the knife wounds, it makes it almost impossible for the attacker to have been anything but left-handed. With the shopkeeper's head pressed to the boxes on shelves against the wall behind the counter, Dr Jones' assessment that there would be too little space to swing the broomhandle would have been correct. A right-handed man, even swinging the broom downwards, would have struck the left side of the face or the top of his head. Were he to have aimed his blow at the right side of Thomas Thomas' face he would have had to swing across his own body and that of the shopkeeper in a right to left arc, and would have almost certainly struck the shelves repeatedly, yet there were no marks on the shelves to indicate they had been hit by a broom handle with two nails sticking out from the end. A left-handed man standing over the shopkeeper however, would be far more likely to have swung the broom handle in an arc parallel to the shelves, connecting repeatedly with the right side of the dying man's face but without ever impacting on the shop's furniture and fittings.

If then the killer was in fact left-handed, where does that leave Tom Morgan? Roughly ten per cent of the population is left-handed. There is good reason why the Latin term for being left-handed – sinister – has come to have such negative connotations in general parlance. It is because those who were – who are left-handed – are an extremely small proportion of society. They are the unusual, the different. If the killer was indeed left-handed then rather than eliminate Morgan, it takes him to the top of a far smaller group of individuals who might possibly have killed Thomas Thomas. None of the other individuals on whom suspicion fell was left-handed. If the killer was left-handed, the list of suspects is reduced to just one.

Had Nicholls been able to convince Dr Jones to remain open-minded with regards the dexterity of the killer, he would surely have been more willing to take seriously the boy Trevor Morgan's claim that he had seen Tom Morgan lurking in the shadows at the bottom or Coronation Arcade near the cellar door of Star Stores at 7pm on the night of the murder. He would no doubt have also pursued further Mrs Williams' adamant recollection that she had not given Morgan a jug of milk at 8pm or the evidence of the Bevans who were in no doubt that Ethel Morgan had not been to the chip shop on Saturday night. If the evidence of Dr Jones no longer seems such a scientific certainty, then the only element in Tom Morgan's favour is the alibi provided by his wife Ethel.

Whatever people's view of her husband, Ethel Morgan was considered beyond reproach. Her employers, John Wilde and his wife, had known her for more than a decade and told Nicholls she was completely trustworthy. "They both state that they have never had any reason to doubt her truthfulness, and it is their opinion that any statement made by her can be relied upon," Nicholls recorded. "She is very highly spoken of," he added – not just by her employers, but also in the wider community.

There was, to Nicholls' knowledge, no evidence or rumour of her ever being anything other than she appeared: an honest, hard-working, God-fearing, chapel-going, shop assistant. She had never stolen, deceived or lied. With Ethel's word that she had been with her husband at home at the time the murder took place, Tom Morgan had nothing to fear.

Ethel Clark met Tom Morgan sometime between 1911 when she first moved to Ammanford and the early days of the Great War. They married at Ammanford Registry Office on September 30, 1915. To the people of the Amman valley, Tom Morgan was a most unlikely hero. He was a most unlikely soldier. He did not go to France nor ever saw active combat. His limp did little to inspire the image of a man who would fight and lay down his life for King and country. He was invalided out of the army on June 10, 1915, having been officially classified unfit for service on May 29 following a medical two days earlier. However, Army Form B 204 – the application for discharge of a recruit as not likely to become an efficient solider, signed by Lieutenant Colonel Gifford at Cardiff tells not even half the story of Tom Morgan's army career.

Had Detective Inspector Nicholls asked any of Garnant's residents how long their neighbour had spent in the Armed Forces it is almost certain his enquiries would have been met with a shrug. The fact Tom and Ethel Morgan only moved to Garnant in 1917, some eighteen months after his discharge, would have been reason enough for the subject to have been of little interest. It was known he had been discharged from the Army and therefore could never have been accused of cowardice. His inability to hold a job underground would have meant he would have been unable to avoid the call to enlist on the grounds of working in a reserved occupation such as mining.

Therefore, it was accepted in the area that he had served and been discharged on medical grounds as unfit for combat. And serve he had – but for far longer than anyone in Garnant might have imagined.

When Tom Morgan was sent to a Borstal institution in January 1910 at the age of 17 years and 4 months, he faced 12 months of a regime designed to turn wayward young delinquents into productive, useful members of society. The most likely prospect for such young men was a career in the army. Their time spent at Borstal was spent under a military-like regime of work, discipline and respect for authority. Morgan and his fellow inmates were not simply encouraged to join the military following the end of their sentence they were actively persuaded to do so as part of Borstal policy. The Army was considered a most suitable means to continue the routines of discipline, respect and regimentation instilled at Borstal and which were considered to have been lacking during the formative years in which they had strayed onto the wrong side of the law. The Army was seen as a way of keeping young men such as Tom Morgan out of trouble.

Morgan was released from Borstal aged 18 years and 4 months in January 1911. The minimum age for recruitment into the Welsh Regiments at the time was 18 years and 6 months. For the next six months he was to remain under the supervision of the Borstal Association until his sentence was finally completed on July 17. During those six months his supervising officer would have continued to push Morgan towards enlisting at the earliest opportunity following the completion of the supervisory section of his sentence. For the next few months, Morgan struggled to find work, his reputation as a thief and a burglar ensuring few employers saw him as a risk worth taking despite his time under the reforming wing of the Borstal Association. He eventually got a job as a miner at the Great Mountain Colliery at Tumble in the Gwendreath Valley, the very western-most edge of the South Wales Coalfield. However, he would not remain underground for more than a few months.

Whether he truly saw it as an opportunity to transform his life, an escape from a career of hard toil or the only choice he had left, Thomas Morgan, miner of 86 High Street, Tumble, joined the First Company, Fourth Battalion, The Welsh Regiment, Territorial Force – 1/4 Welsh (TF) – at the village recruiting station on May 17, 1912. His enlistment documentation gives his age as 18 years and eight months though he was in fact 19 years and eight months. Morgan signed up for four years service. In 1912, the soldiers of 1/4th Battalion, The Welsh Regiment, Territorial Force, were, by decree, only to be posted within the United Kingdom and could only to bear arms within the UK's shores.

Clause G of the Attestation Form signed by Morgan and all other recruits declared: "That you will be liable to serve in any place in the United Kingdom without further agreement, but not any place outside the United Kingdom unless you voluntarily undertake to do so."

Such an undertaking would have had little concern for Tom Morgan. He was no longer welcome in the places he called home anyway. When he signed his name on Army forms E501 and E501/a it is unlikely he gave little thought to the future or international affairs. Certainly he would have seen little reason to have been alarmed in the clauses preceding Clause G.

Clause E: "That when a proclamation has been issued, in the case of imminent national danger or great emergency, calling out the first class Army Reserve you will become liable to be embodied."

Clause F: "That, if your term of four years' service expires when a proclamation ordering the Army Reserve to be called out on permanent service is in force, you may be required to prolong your service for a further period not exceeding 12 months."

At his Army medical, Tom Morgan was declared fit, healthy and suitable for duty with a territorial force. His height was measured at five feet and five inches – two inches taller than the minimum five-foot-three. Morgan was given service number 3939 and underwent his basic training between the end of May and August 11, 1912. He spent most of the remainder of the year and 1913 moving between camps around Wales. Then the world began to change. The assassination of Archduke Franz Ferdinand of Austro-Hungary in Bosnia on June 28, 1914, set in motion a series of events which would throw millions of lives into turmoil, including that of Tom Morgan. The killing of some

European aristocrat, of whom Morgan like so many others had never previously heard, put the United Kingdom on a war footing, and the 4th Welsh territorial force were moved to camp at Porthmadog on July 26. Eight days later, British troops were ordered to mobilise. Clause E of Form 501/a suddenly had meaning and on August 5, 1914, Tom Morgan, like the rest of his battalion, was 'embodied'.

For soldiers such as Tom Morgan who had joined the Army long before the murder of an unknown minor royal in some far-flung country, the idea of being sent to some foreign field to fight and die must have been horrific. This was not a case of signing up to kill for King and country or even being called up, these soldiers found themselves already in an army that was preparing to take part in what would become the greatest conflict the world had ever known. For the likes of Morgan in the Territorial Forces there was one saving grace however – Clause G of the Attestation Form signed more than two years earlier. The form was unequivocal. Morgan and his fellow soldiers were "liable to serve in any place in the United Kingdom without further agreement, but not any place outside the United Kingdom unless you voluntarily undertake to do so". Tom Morgan had no intention whatsoever of volunteering for anything. During the remainder of 1914 and early 1915, members of the 1/4 Welsh Regiment (TF) guarded the Home Front while others went to Flanders. By spring 1915, that too was about to change. Members of the 1/4 (TF) received word that they would be forced to choose between joining the front line in northern France or remaining as part of the territorial force which would see them remain stationed only at British bases. Those young men who agreed to transfer from the terri-torial to the expeditionary force and head for France would remain in 1/4, those who chose to remain UK-bound would transfer to 2/4 Battalion, The Welsh Regiment. It was clear that any able-bodied soldier who wished to avoid being labelled a coward was expected to sign up and join their comrades overseas. Meanwhile, those members who were transferred to 2/4 would be stationed in Pembroke Dock and take up roles as recruiters and trainers for the Expeditionary Force. Tom Morgan had no intention of going to France, but he was not overly keen on moving to Pembrokeshire either, having begun his relationship with Ethel, the woman who would become his wife. His situation was further complicated by the fact that, having served almost three full years of his four-year term, he was all but certain to be retained for a further 12 months. Morgan also must have found himself wondering whether the terms of the contract of transfer to 2/4 would be binding. It was obvious that the Army was becoming increasing desperate for more men at the front line and, with two more years of service ahead of him, he must have questioned whether he too would inevitably be destined for the trenches. Given time to consider their options, the men of 1/4 (TF) spent the last weeks of March and early April deciding their futures ahead of the April 20 deadline. Tom Morgan had no doubt in his mind as to what he would do. Despite a previously unblemished record during his first three years of service – surely the first time in his life he had avoided any scrapes with authority or the law, Morgan reverted to his former self. On March 26, he was sentenced to month's imprisonment for disobeying a direct order and insubordination.

His military records reads: "Awarded 28 days detention (1) returning to billet after being warned not to (2) using obscene language to a non-commissioned officer." He was due for release on April 22 – two days after the deadline to choose between remaining with the territorial or transferring to the expeditionary force. However, Private Morgan chose not to do his time quietly. "Award 14 days detention from expiration of present term – urinating in cell while undergoing detention," reads the note recorded on his file.

Having spent two years and ten months as the perfect soldier, Tom Morgan went completely off the rails three weeks before he would be forced to choose between setting sail for the killing fields of France or facing the very real possibility of being branded a coward by remaining on home soil. Reading between the lines, it seems as if Tom Morgan was making every effort to prove to his superiors that he was unfit to be a soldier in the hope that he might be booted out of the regiment. The Army however had far bigger things to consider. Rather than being thrown out of the 1/4, Tom Morgan was forced to make his choice , and on April 20 he opted to remain within the UK and transferred to 2/4 ahead of posting to the training barracks at Pembroke Dock, some 50 miles west of Ethel and the Amman Valley. He was given the new service number 200777. His decision was little more than an effort to buy himself some time. On April 20 – the day he was due to arrive in Pembrokeshire, his new commanding officer declared Thomas Morgan, 200777, absent without leave. Ten days later – the minimum period of time permissible under British Army regulations – Tom Morgan was officially declared a deserter. He had never arrived at Pembroke Dock.

The penalty for desertion, even from the Territorial Force, was severe, both within the Army and in the eyes of the public. Morgan was all too aware he would be unable to run and hide. A man of his age with no family or job and not enlisted in the army would have been noticed. Inevitably the military police would have eventually tracked him down and returned him to barracks to face punishment. He would need to use all his guile to escape detection – and the scheme he dreamt up was audacious in both its simplicity and its cunning.

On April 23, three days after he had been due to arrive in Pembroke Dock and seven days before he was officially declared a deserter, a young man with a limp walked into the Swansea recruiting office of Third Battalion, The Welsh Regiment. The young man gave his name as Conway Morgan and listed his address as 18 Walters Road, Ammanford. He gave his age as 21 years and seven months and said his occupation was miner. As a God-fearing chapel-goer, Conway Morgan asked to join the newly-formed Temperance Company – set up the previous December for those souls of strong moral virtue who wished to completely avoid the demon drink. When the young miner arrived in Swansea for his medical he must have done so with every expectation that he would be rejected. He walked with a pronounced limp and when measured by the medical officer, stood at five feet one and three-quarters, one-and-a-quarter inches below the minimum requirement to join the British Army at the outbreak of the war and before. Had the new recruit been able stand up straight, or had his limp not forced him to slump to one side, he would undoubtedly have passed the basic height requirements. It will never be known whether he was aware that the previous December the Army had agreed to relax its height restrictions and create what became known as the Bantam Battalions, for men standing between five-foot tall and five-foot-three. The introduction of the Bantams had come following demands from Welsh miners, short and stocky by nature, who though able-bodied and more than capable of fighting were deemed too short for war. Perhaps the new recruit had specifically sought to join the Bantams or possibly he had been stunned into silence upon learning that had he attempted to sign up four months earlier he would have been immediately rejected. Now though he was welcome to enlist and join the war effort.

What is absolutely certain is that the Conway Morgan who walked into the Swansea recruiting office to join 3 Welsh on April 23, 1915, was undoubtedly Thomas Conway Morgan, who had deserted 2/4 Welsh just three days earlier. Conway Morgan gave his date of birth as September 15, 1893, – one year to the day younger than Tom Morgan. He gave his birthplace as Llangadock in the Towy Valley – the same small village where Tom Morgan had been born, and he gave his next of kin as E Morgan, 18 Walters Road, Ammanford. Tom Morgan's mother Emily had moved to 18 Walters Road some time between his first enlistment in May 1912 and his first period of home leave in May, 1913.

Presumably much to his great surprise and disappointment, Conway Morgan was formally accepted into 3 Welsh (Temperance Co) on April 26, 1915. When asked whether he had undergone any military training or served with any regiment of the British Army previously he said that he had not. He was sent to Newton Camp, Porthcawl, to undergo his basic training. The company he had joined was no territorial force, 3 Welsh (Temperance Co) was destined for the front. It is all but certain that Morgan had expected his application to join 3 Welsh to be rejected – either due to his height or the foot injury, which caused his limp. There is no record whatsoever from his file while a member of 1/4 Welsh of him having any such injury. There is no record of any incident or accident which might have caused it. On the day he was expected to choose whether to head for the front or go west to Pembrokeshire, he was deemed fit and able. Sometime between April 20 and April 23 he sustained the injury which, he must have assumed, would exclude him from military service. T Lewis Jones, the medical examining officer for 3 Welsh recruitment at Swansea, clearly thought it superficial and made no note of the problem. He listed Conway Morgan's general health as "good" and in the section set aside for slight defects or injuries wrote "none". Tom Conway Morgan must have been horrified. There is no doubt that Morgan's foot injury was real. How it came about remains a mystery; whether it was caused by accident or self-inflicted no record shows, but it was certainly to plague him for the remainder of his life. Morgan arrived at Porthcawl on May 5 in a state of genuine panic. The only option to him was to play on his damaged foot as much as possible and bide his time. The tactic was eventually to pay off and his injuries were brought to the attention of his commanding officer. Dr T Lewis Jones was summoned to re-examine the recruit and, on May 27, in the presence of Major T Anderson, Conway Morgan was found to have ankylosis of the big toe and second toe of the left foot due to recent injury. He suffered inflammation and rigidity of the joints. It was thought unlikely that it would ever heal. A note on Morgan's medical file reads: "Quite unfit for military service. This man was lame when he enlisted." On June 4, Conway Morgan was finally discharged from the Army with a further note included on his file to withhold the six pence and two shillings normally payable to the recruiting officer.

Thomas Conway Morgan's elaborate plan had paid off. Should he ever be confronted by military police and accused of desertion or labelled a coward, he need only produce his signed copy of form B204 – Application for Discharge of a Recruit as not likely to become an efficient soldier. The document proved he had actively attempted to enlist and had been rejected during basic training as a man who was "lame when he enlisted".

It is no surprise then that the people of Garnant knew little of Tom Morgan's Army background. The one person – apart from Morgan himself – who did know his full military history, was Ethel, his wife. The couple married less than four months after his discharge from 3 Welsh. But they had been certainly been an item when he was a serving soldier with 1/4 (TF) and when he was under military detention. They were also an item when he

enlisted with 3 Welsh and when he went into basic training for a
second time at Porthcawl. It is inconceivable that Ethel Clark did
not know her fiancée was a deserter. It is equally inconceivable
that she had been unaware that he had enlisted in 3 Welsh under
a different name and a false date of birth. Ethel Clark was part
of the conspiracy by which Tom Morgan, deserter, became
Conway Morgan, willing new recruit. She may have even tended
the injury suffered between April 20 and April 23 which would
ultimately save him from the trenches. Ethel Clark knew her
man was a liar, a fraudster, a deserter and a coward. Whether she
cared, or whether she thought this man – a decade her junior –
was her only chance at marriage and happiness, she knew full
well what he was and what he had done. On September 30 at
Ammanford Registry Office, she said "I do" and became Ethel
Morgan, wife of Thomas Conway Morgan. Ethel Morgan nee
Clark was not the honest, law-abiding, truthful woman that she
claimed to be. She had played a significant part in the biggest lie
her husband ever told.

When Priscilla Davies looked out from her house at Lamb
Buildings at just before 11pm on February 12 to see her neighbours tending the last remnants of a small bonfire, she was
looking into the garden of Old Anchor House. She knew the
house well. She had, after all, been born inside it. When she
stared out in the darkness of that cold winter night and saw the
flickering flames she asked herself why on earth her neighbours
would be burning rags at such a time of night. Had she taken a
moment to step outside to look more closely, she might then
have realised that they were not burning rags, but clothes – a
man's shirt, a jacket and a pair of trousers. From her window she
could not make out the items, nor could she see that they were
all soaked with blood. There was much she could not make out
in the darkness, but Priscilla Davies could clearly see her neighbours – the couple to whom her family had rented out her
childhood home for 18 shillings a month. She could clearly see
and recognise the figures of Tom and Ethel Morgan.

Had Detective Inspector George Nicholls known that Ethel
Morgan had been so willing to lie and cover for her husband;
had he known that throughout their entire married life she had
lived behind a veil of lies as much as had her spouse; had he

known that when it came to protecting Tom her virtue counted for little; had he known that within hours of the murder of Thomas Thomas she and Tom were burning blood-soaked clothes, he might have been less willing to accept the Wildes' blind faith in her honesty and integrity.

"They both state that they have never had any reason to doubt her truthfulness, and it is their opinion that any statement made by her can be relied upon," Nicholls had written in his final report on the case. If he had known the truth of Tom Morgan's military past he would surely have dismissed the alibi she provided for her husband more quickly than he had the evidence of Mrs Williams or the shop assistant Trevor Morgan. If Priscilla Davies had connected the fire in the night with the killing just a short walk down the valley road and told the man from Scotland Yard, perhaps Nicholls would have sent Canning to search the garden for charred remains rather than the house for broken buttons. If he had known the lengths to which Ethel Morgan might go to protect her husband, he might in fact have caught the man who killed Thomas Thomas on February 12, 1921. Had George Nicholls known any of these things he would have caught the murderer at the Star.

Chapter Seventeen:
Denouement

ALTHOUGH THE KILLER OF Thomas Thomas would ultimately elude him, George Nicholls' career did not suffer any major setback due to his failure in West Wales. A year after his return to London he was promoted to the rank of Chief Inspector. On May 21, 1926, he was made Superintendent, a move that would see him heralded in the national press as one of New Scotland Yard's "big five" – the quintet of Britain's most important and influential police officers. He was made an MBE in the 1932 New Year honours list and on August 8 that year, thirty-two years after he had been made detective and in the department in which he had spent almost his entire career, George Robert Nicholls, the nightwatchman's son, was appointed Chief Constable of the Criminal Investigation Department. Nicholls retired from the Metropolitan Police in 1934 after thirty-five years service. Despite a glittering career that saw him arrest international fraudsters, forge links with the police forces of all major European countries, operate as a spy-catcher during the First World War and lead the most famous department of the most famous police force in the world, he would never close the case on the killing of Thomas Thomas . The murder at the Star Stores could never be considered Nicholls' biggest case and there were far greater failings and much, much greater successes throughout his career, but the murderer of a shopkeeper in a small West Wales mining village remains one that got away.

In the long years that followed the events of February 12, 1921, the story of the murder at Star Stores slipped ever further into the realms of legend and old wives' tale. Garnant parents used it as a tale to frighten their children and throughout the 1940s and 50s, the youngsters of the village, in their turn, played a game they called Murder at the Star. As clear memory of that night and the days that followed was slowly lost, only one constant remained. During the course of researching this book more than a dozen people have come forward, all claiming to know who killed Thomas Thomas. Each has said without fail that Mountstephens was the killer. To support the claim, a few of those said that Mountstephens and his family had disappeared the night after the killing, another claimed they had run inside a week and the remainder all stated that the Mountstephens family had escaped justice and emigrated to America within a month or two of the murder. In the essay that first inspired me to research the story, *A Long Time Between Murders*, Owen Jones – himself a Garnant native who, though born nine years after the event, grew up two doors along from the Star – wrote that Mountstephens and his family emigrated soon after the murder to Australia. Owen was at least half right. The Mountstephens family certainly did leave Garnant and start a new life for themselves in Australia, but it was no moonlit flit as the common belief now holds.

On September 21, 1929, more than eight years after the murder of his friend and lodger, Thomas Mountstephens along with his wife Lily and youngest son, 18-year-old William, set sail from Liverpool on the White Star Line vessel *Themistocles,* calling at Tenerife, South Africa and finally Australia. Arthur Mountstephens, the couple's elder son, had arrived in Fremantle in Western Australia almost exactly twelve months earlier, having first spent six weeks on a UK Government-sponsored training programme teaching young men the skills necessary to farm the baked earth of the outback. Clearly, Arthur found life Down Under to his liking and he encouraged his parents and brother to join him. Thomas Hooper Mountstephens' death was registered in Perth, Australia, in 1966. Lily's death was recorded at the same registrar's office three years later.

There is no question that the Mountstephens family ran away from Garnant, but it was certainly not to escape detection for a murder which occurred eight years earlier and was little more than a fading record in the annals of Scotland Yard and the Carmarthenshire Constabulary by the time they left West Wales. But while the official documents viewed the murder at the Star as a closed case in all but name, for the residents of Garnant it remained very much alive. So much so, that Owen Jones, born the year after Thomas and Lily set sail, spent his childhood hearing tales of how Mountstephens killed his lodger. In *A Long Time Between Murders*, Owen – contemplating the reasons for the Mountstephens' departure – states: "whether they did so out of guilt or to escape persecution, at this distance there is no way of telling". Thomas Hooper Mountstephens may well have been aloof, perhaps even arrogant and quite possibly considered himself better than the men he worked alongside, but he was certainly not guilty of the crime of murder. Mountstephens did not killer his lodger, his friend. Once that possibility is eliminated, Owen Jones is left with only one alternative.

Morgan Walter Jeffreys was considered a suspect by many of the people of Garnant during the early days of the investigation thanks to his presence at the rear of the Star, his contradictory statements regarding the night of the murder and his strange behaviour the following day. A further reason why suspicion had been aimed his direction was the use of a knife as weapon. Jeffreys was a butcher and though his early life was spent as a grocer, his arrival in Garnant saw him set up shop as a man who knew how to handle a blade. However, Nicholls never seriously considered him a suspect of any real merit thanks in the main to his age and fading health. The policeman was correct. Less than three years after the murder, Morgan Walter Jeffreys died. He was sixty years of age and his health finally did what the trials and tribulations of his life had failed to do. He died on February 12, 1924 – three years to the day of the murder of Thomas Thomas – of a cerebral haemorrhage, a stroke. His son Morgan was at his side in the family home Glanynant when he died. The shadow of the murder had clung to him in the final few years of his life with some in the village still believing he had played some role in the murder, but though his actions were suspicious on the night of the killing and the next day, Morgan Walter Jeffreys played no part in the murder.

Sergeant Thomas Richards retired from the Carmarthenshire Constabulary at the age of 60 on June 26, 1936, after almost forty-two years of service. The murder of Thomas Thomas in 1921 was the only homicide he would ever work on. Following his promotion to Sergeant in April 1913 he was transferred to

Cwmaman the following month and remained there for the remainder of his career. After leaving the force, he moved to a house in the village where he would remain for the rest of his life. In 1935 he received the King George Jubilee Medal. When George Nicholls returned to London and rose to the pinnacle of the Metropolitan Police, his failure to catch the killer of Thomas Thomas became a minor and rarely mentioned footnote in his long, illustrious service. For the uniformed officer who he admired and respected in the West Wales mining village however, the unsolved case would be perhaps the defining moment of his career. When his imminent retirement was reported in the *Amman Valley Chronicle*, the five paragraphs which summed up his four decades in uniform, highlighted his time on duty at industrial disputes across Wales, his attendance at royal visits by Princes and the King, but made no mention of the biggest case of his career. The following week, after his departure from the force, the same paper reminded readers that Sergeant Richards had been the man on duty the night a killer got away with murder.

On April 14, 1921 – 63 days after the murder at the Star, Deputy Chief Constable John Evans, the Carmarthenshire Constabulary's most senior officer directly involved with the case, retired from the force as part of the introduction of the Government's Retirement Age Bill which was then passing through Parliament. With the departure of Deputy Chief Constable Evans, the investigation into the murder at the Star formally, if not officially, came to a close. Despite also reaching the age of retirement in 1921, Chief Constable William Picton Phillipps, who had taken over the role as head of the Carmarthenshire Constabulary from his father in 1908, remained in post for another nineteen years until his retirement in 1940. The murder of the Garnant shopkeeper would remain the only unsolved murder to have occurred within his jurisdiction during his thirty-two years at the head of the Carmarthenshire Constabulary.

Thomas Conway Hewitt Morgan, the man who spent a year in Borstal as a teen, deserted from the army and earned himself a reputation as a thief and a fraud, also got away with murder – literally. When interviewed by Nicholls, Morgan, the man whose deformed hand saved him from the close scrutiny that might well have sent him to the gallows, claimed he planned to buy himself a horse and cart to sell fish and vegetables in the Amman Valley. In fact, he went one better. By 1928, when he stood in for his sick father to give his sister Fanny away in marriage, Tom Morgan was manager – perhaps even owner – of the Supply Stores, Ammanford, a grocery outlet to rival both the Star Supply Stores branch in the town and Wilde's greengrocers where Ethel had worked for a decade-and-a-half and whose faith in his wife ensured his alibi went untested. Tom Morgan, the man who spent his entire life on the wrong side of the law, appeared to earn himself a place in the establishment of the Amman Valley. The man, who at the age of 11 was bound over for stealing boxes of chocolates from the town store, had become a shopkeeper, a businessman, a productive member of society. But for a man like Tom Morgan, the outfit of upstanding citizen was an uncomfortable fit. At some point during the next decade Ethel left him. Whether it was before or after he lost the business is not known, but lose it he did. And the woman who had remained by his side throughout his desertion from the Army and the murder of Thomas Thomas at last abandoned him. Whether the murder which hung over both of them like a shadow was the thing that tore them apart will never be known. What is known is that by the winter of 1946, Tom Morgan was alone, he was in poverty and he was homeless. With nowhere else to go, He spent the autumn sleeping at his brother's house at 13 Quarry Terrace, Pantyffynnon – a small village on the outskirts of Ammanford which gradually became absorbed as the town spread. On Friday, November 29, Tom Morgan, jobless and broke, went to pay his weekly visit to the town labour exchange. There was no work on offer for a one-handed labourer with a reputation as a thief. He returned to Quarry Terrace where, whether tormented by the evil of his past or distraught at his current situation, he made his way to the shed at the bottom of the garden where coal was stored with a length of rope in his hand. On a cold November afternoon with little to look forward to, Thomas Conway Hewitt Morgan hanged himself. The Coroner who investigated the death ruled it suicide – asphyxia due to self-hanging while the balance of his mind was disturbed. Whether it was the image of the dead shopkeeper lying blood-soaked on the floor which caused the imbalance, we shall never know.

Chapter Eighteen:
Postscript

WHEN I FIRST BEGAN researching the murder at Star Stores I did so in the hope that I might somehow find it possible to prove once and for all that Thomas Hooper Mountstephens had killed Thomas Thomas on February 12, 1921. Every person I had spoken with was sure that the man from Glanyrafon Villas had killed the shopkeeper – it was simply that the police had never been able to prove it. Every man and woman I spoke with said the same: "The murderer was the landlord, Mountstephens." Each person had been told by their parents and grandparents. The rumour had been retold so many times it had to all intents and purposes become a truth. The article where I first learned of the crime, Owen Jones' excellent *A Long Time Between Murders* stated the same thing. It was Mountstephens.

Everyone who came forward to name Mountstephens as the killer also offered up the second morsel as further evidence of his guilt. The belief – to this day in Garnant – that the entire Mountstephens family disappeared overnight. One day they were there, the next they were gone. What further proof of guilt could be required? The tale however could not have been further from the truth and the more I researched the Amman Valley of the time the more I realised that Thomas Hooper Mountstephens was an innocent man, branded a killer by village gossip and pub rumour. I have also repeatedly asked myself who was the man who approached John Thomas in the Farmers Arms. The description is so vague that the stationmaster could have been talking about almost any of Garnant's male residents at that time, but the physical description certainly does fit Thomas Conway Hewitt Morgan.

As I continued scratching away at the surface of the crime, gathering what information I could from police files, newspaper clippings, county archives and personal documents, I came to believe that rather than running across the ocean to avoid detection for his crime, Thomas Mountstephens took his family abroad to escape the stigma, the accusatory fingers, the whispered comments as they passed by in the street. It remains my view that Thomas Mountstephens was driven out of Garnant by the false accusations he could never shake off. Researching the murder at the Star became not a bid to prove him guilty of the crime, but instead an effort to finally clear his name.

It was only once I had finally convinced myself that Mountstephens was not the killer that I seriously began to consider who else might possibly have committed murder. There always remained the chance that some outsider had killed Thomas Thomas, but the facts of the case and the culprit's knowledge of his victim and his habits all pointed to a killer who shopped at the Star. I had been made aware that there were some rumours that Phoebe Jones had had a lover, and it was this unknown person who killed Thomas Thomas, either during a failed robbery or as revenge for some slight or insult the shop manager had aimed at his secret love. There was also a brief rumour that Thomas Thomas had made either inappropriate remarks or acted improperly towards his first hand and his killing was the result of the outraged lover. Such a claim would seem absurd given what we know of Thomas Thomas. Nicholls in his case files never once considered Phoebe Jones a suspect. Given her alibi, her concern when she returned from the dance and her horror at the discovery of the body, neither did I. One by one the potential suspects, fell away until all that was left was Tom Morgan. The more I discovered about the man – things Nicholls could not have known – the more convinced I became that he was the killer. It was only then that the evidence of Dr Jones was seriously called into question. And once the questioning began it seemed to become all too apparent that, despite his undoubted medical expertise, the doctor had read the crime scene incorrectly. He started from the assumption that because the cut to the throat seemed, on paper at least, the most deadly of the wounds, it must therefore have been the last. That simple assumption made it all but impossible to solve the murder at the Star.

The village of Garnant is not accustomed to violent crime.

There have only ever been two murders – the killing of Thomas Thomas in 1921 and the murder of a chef by his employer who discovered that his worker had taken more than just a passing fancy to his wife. More than eighty years passed between the two killings. The perpetrator of the second crime was caught almost immediately. Garnant, and the whole of the Amman Valley, is a beautiful peaceful place. Murders have no place there. The residents are friendly, cheerful and always happy to put themselves out to help anyone and everyone who happens along into such a gloriously beautiful little corner of Wales. If this book has, to the satisfaction of those who read it, finally solved the one black mark on the history of this wonderful little village then it will have served its purpose. The hundreds of hours spent in libraries, archives and museums, straining my eyes at computer screens long into the night or attempting to decipher 93-year-old handwriting in fading ink will have all been worth it. The greatest achievement however will be the knowledge that finally, once and for all, the name of Thomas Hooper Mountstephens has at last been cleared of this heinous crime and the true identity of the murderer at the Star revealed.

The Author

Steve Adams is an experienced journalist who became the editor of the *South Wales Guardian* in 2014. Originally from Pembrokeshire, he was educated at Cardiff University and attended the University of Central Lancashire's print journalism course. Since then he has worked on the *Western Telegraph, South Wales Guardian* and the *Western Mail,* as well as acting on a freelance basis for national newspapers, magazines and journals as well as various websites.

Steve Adams first became aware of the unsolved murder of Thomas Thomas while researching feature ideas for the *South Wales Guardian.* It was clear to him that the story of the murder, both in terms of the case and as a metaphor for the changing nature of Welsh life in the early 1900s, had the strength and depth to sustain a far longer piece of work than a short newspaper feature. His research and contacts allowed him to discover far more of the background and subsequent mythologising of the murder than has ever before been reported, including the eventual revealing of the killer's identity.